ONE MINUTE REFERENCE

WordPerfect® 6 for Windows™

*by Joseph R. Levy and
Jennifer Fulton*

alpha books

A Division of Prentice Hall Computer Publishing
201 West 103rd Street, Indianapolis, IN 46290 USA

International Standard Book Number: 1-56761-283-0
Library of Congress Catalog Card Number: 93-71738

95 94 93   8 7 6 5 4 3 2 1

Interpretation of the printing code: the rightmost number of the first series of numbers is the year of the book's printing; the rightmost number of the second series of numbers is the number of the book's printing. For example, a printing code of 93-1 shows that the first printing of the book occurred in 1993.

Publisher: *Marie Butler-Knight*
Associate Publisher: *Lisa A. Bucki*
Managing Editor: *Elizabeth Keaffaber*
Acquisitions Manager: *Stephen R. Poland*
Development Editor: *Mary Cole Rack*
Copy Editor: *Audra Gable*
Cover Design: *Jay Corpus*
Index: *Jennifer Eberhardt*
Production: *Gary Adair, Diana Bigham, Tim Cox, Meshell Dinn, Mark Enochs, Tim Groeling, Howard Jones, Beth Rago, Carrie Roth, Marc Shecter*

Screen reproductions in this book were created by means of the program Collage Plus from Inner Media, Inc., Hollis, NH.

Printed in the United States of America

Special thanks to Kelly Oliver for ensuring the technical accuracy of this book.

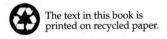

Contents

Introduction

The One Minute Reference WordPerfect 6 for Windows *offers unique help by providing short, clear step-by-step instructions for when you are in a hurry. This book is designed for the person who:*

- Doesn't have time to flip through a large manual.

- Wants only the steps that are necessary to accomplish a task, but not a lot of text.

- Wants no-nonsense instructions to complete a task.

   The *One Minute Reference WordPerfect 6 for Windows* gives easy-to-understand steps for the tasks you need to accomplish quickly.

Conventions Used in This Book

This book offers several design features to make its use as simple as possible. These features include:

- *Alphabetical organization*   Tasks are organized in alphabetical order for quick-and-easy fingertip access of important topics.

- *Keycap column*   All steps are concise, with the keys you need to press or information you need to type to accomplish a task listed to the right of the step.

Keys to press are shown as *keycaps*
like this ....⏎

Information to type is shown in bold,
italic text like this ....***text***

- *Optional steps*   Some steps may begin with
  the word **(Optional)**. If you do not want to
  use this option, just skip the step!

- *Key combinations*   Key combinations are
  often used to accomplish a task. For example, if you are asked to press Alt + A,
  press the **Alt** key and the **A** at the same time.

- *Selection letters*   Each menu and command
  has one underlined letter in its name, which
  you use when making keyboard selections.
  Menu and command names in this book
  show the selection letters in bold print.

- *Multiple options*   If you see an "*or*" in a
  step, use the method of your choice for that
  step.

- Some steps will take more than one
  keypress or action. When this is the
  case, you'll see the actions listed
  vertically ....Alt + A

This icon points out extra information about WordPerfect 6.0 for Windows or techniques for using WordPerfect for Windows' 6.0 features that you may find valuable.

This icon gives examples to help you understand how to use the feature being discussed.

This icon features quick steps for accomplishing the same task with a mouse.

WordPerfect 6.0 for Windows Basics

WordPerfect 6.0 for Windows is a word processing package and much more. Revitalize those old documents by formatting them quickly and cleanly. Create office memos, pictures, letter templates, labels, and graphs, or add your company logo as a watermark on letterhead. You can even embed complex mathematical equations with specialized characters into your documents or compile indexes and tables of contents—all without leaving the WordPerfect program. WordPerfect for Windows makes word processing easy: you select menu items rather than typing complex commands. But don't race to lay out your first document just yet! Before you can take advantage of WordPerfect, you must learn some basics.

To start WordPerfect 6.0 for Windows, do the following:

1. At the DOS prompt, type .... **WIN**

2. Press ....⏎

3. Open the program group that contains the WordPerfect 6.0 icon by double-clicking on it (usually this is the "WPWin 6.0" program group).

4. Double-click on the **WpWin 6.0** icon.

5. Wait for the WordPerfect screen to appear.

TIP

You must have Windows installed in order to run the WordPerfect 6.0 for Windows program.

If you have not installed WordPerfect 6.0 for Windows on your computer, follow these steps to install it:

1. Put the WordPerfect 6.0 for Windows Install 1 disk in drive A or drive B.

2. Select the Windows Program Manager.

3. Select the **F**ile menu.

4. Select **R**un.

5. Type **a:install** (or **b:install**).

6. Read the on-screen instructions and follow the prompts until a message appears and tells you the installation is complete.

7. Click on **OK** or press **Enter**.

8. The WPWIN 6.0 program group appears. Double-click on the **WPWIN 6.0** icon.

The WordPerfect 6.0 for Windows title screen appears for a few moments, and then WordPerfect displays an empty document you can begin working on right away.

Parts of a WordPerfect 6.0 for Windows Screen

The WordPerfect 6.0 for Windows screen contains several distinctive elements which you won't see in DOS. Here's a brief summary:

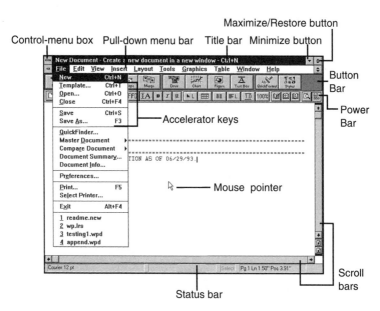

Figure 1   A WordPerfect for Windows screen.

- **Title bar**   Located along the top of a window or screen, the title bar shows the name of the window or program.

- **Minimize and Maximize buttons** Located at the upper right corner of a window or screen, these buttons look like a down arrow and up arrow and are used to alter a window's size. The Minimize button shrinks the window to the size of an icon. The Maximize button expands the window to fill the screen. When maximized, a window contains a double-arrow Restore button, which returns the window to its original size.

- **Control-menu box** Located in the upper left corner of a window or screen, the Control-menu box looks like a box with a hyphen in it. When you click on it, a pull-down menu appears, offering size and location controls for the window.

- **Pull-down menu bar** Located below the title bar, this bar contains a list of the pull-down menus available in the program.

- **Button Bar** The Button Bar shown in Figure 1 is one of twelve. Instead of selecting a feature from a menu, you can access it directly by clicking with the mouse on its icon in a Button Bar. To switch to a different Button Bar, click with the right mouse button on the displayed Button Bar, and select a different one from the QuickMenu.

- **Power Bar**   Contains the most frequently used text editing and text layout features in WordPerfect for Windows. Use it for quick access to the features represented by the icons on it.

- **Status bar**   Displays information, such as the current page and line number, font, status of the Insert key, and so on.

- **Mouse pointer**   When you use a mouse, the mouse pointer appears on-screen (usually as an arrow as in the figure). You control it by moving the mouse.

- **Scroll bars**   Scroll bars appear at the bottom or right side of a window, or both. When a window contains more information than it can display, use the scroll arrows on each end of the scroll bar to move through the document slowly. Use the scroll boxes to move quickly from one screen to the next.

- **Accelerator keys**   Often you will see keystroke letters and numbers to the right of a command name. These keys can be used from the keyboard to access a command directly without having to open a menu and then select the command from it.

Using a Mouse

To work efficiently in WordPerfect, you should use a mouse. You press the mouse buttons and move the mouse to accomplish tasks quickly. The following list defines the actions you need to be able to perform with the mouse:

- *Point* means to move the mouse pointer onto the specified item on-screen.

- *Click on an item* means to move the pointer onto the specified item and press the mouse button once. Unless specified otherwise, use the left mouse button.

- *Double-click on an item* means to move the mouse pointer onto the specified item and click the mouse button twice quickly.

- *Drag* means to move the mouse pointer onto the specified item, and then press and hold down the mouse button while moving the mouse. Release the mouse button only when you have placed the specified item where you want it.

Choosing Menus and Commands

The pull-down menu bar contains various menus from which you can select commands. All menu names and commands have one underlined letter.

This is called the selection letter. *You press it to choose a menu or command with the keyboard when you do not use a mouse. (Selection letters are indicated in **bold** in this book.) To open a menu and choose a command, use either the mouse steps or the keyboard steps described here.*

Mouse Steps

1. Click on the menu name on the menu bar.

2. Click on the desired command.

Keyboard Steps

1. Choose the menu .... Alt + *selection letter*

2. Choose the command .... *selection letter*

TIP

Notice that some commands are followed by key names, such as Ctrl+O (for the Open File command). These are called **accelerator keys**. You can use these keys to perform the specified command without even opening the menu.

Usually, when you select a command, the command is performed immediately, However:

• If the command name appears gray (rather than black), the command is unavailable at the moment, and you cannot choose it.

• If the command name is followed by an arrow, selecting that command will cause another menu to appear, from which you select an option.

- If the command name is followed by an ellipsis (three dots), selecting it will cause a dialog box to appear. You'll learn about dialog boxes later in this introduction.

Using Button Bars, the Power Bar, and QuickMenus

WordPerfect provides twelve Button Bars, which contain groups of icons relating to specific activities, such as changing page layout or page settings, adding tables, and creating graphics. The buttons are activated by clicking on them with the mouse. By changing from one Button Bar to another, you can quickly perform related commands.

There is also a Power Bar, which includes icons for basic activities, such as opening or saving a file, cutting and pasting text, spell checking, and printing.

QuickMenus are pop-up menus which are opened by clicking the right mouse button in different areas of the screen. The QuickMenu commands relate to the activity you are currently performing.

Navigating Dialog Boxes

*A dialog box is WordPerfect's way of requesting additional information. To open a dialog box, choose a command from one of the menus on the menu bar. Press **Tab** to move from option to option inside a dialog box. Each dialog box contains one or more of the following elements:*

- *List boxes* display available choices. To select an item from a list, click on it. If the entire list is not visible, use the scroll bar to view the items in the list.

- *Drop-down lists* are similar to list boxes, but only one item in the list is shown. To see the rest of the items, click on the down arrow in the right of the box. To select an item from the list, click on it.

- *Text boxes* allow you to type an entry. To activate a text box, click inside it. To edit an existing entry, use the arrow keys to move the cursor and press the Delete or Backspace keys to delete existing characters. Then type your correction.

- *Check boxes* allow you to select one or more items in a group of options. For example, if you are styling text, you can select Bold and Italic to have the text appear in both bold and italic type. Click on a check box to activate it. To deactivate the option, clear the check box by clicking on it again.

- *Option buttons* are like check boxes, but you can select only one option button in a group. Selecting one button deselects any option that is already selected. Click on an option button to activate it.

- *Command buttons* execute (or cancel) the command once you have made your selection in the dialog box. To select a command button, click on it.

To close a dialog box, make your decisions and click **Close** or **OK**. To cancel your selections, click **Cancel** or press **Esc**.

Navigating Documents

At any time, you may have one or more documents open and layered on top of one another. These documents are all available, and you can click on the Window menu and select a document to switch to it.

Selecting and Deselecting Text

You will use these techniques throughout the program to define the portion of the text that you want to move, delete, edit, enhance, overtype, or copy. The text that you select will be highlighted.

Mouse Steps

Here are two ways to use the mouse to select text in WordPerfect:

- Place the mouse pointer at either end of the text you want to select. Press and hold the left mouse button while you drag the pointer across the text to the other end. Then release the button. The text is highlighted.

- Double-click to select one word. Triple-click to select a sentence. Quadruple-click to select an entire paragraph.

To deselect the text, click the mouse button outside the block of selected text.

MOUSE

There is another way to select text using the mouse and the invisible selection bar in the left margin of the document. When the mouse pointer moves into the selection bar, it changes the direction in which it points from upward to the left to upward to the right. With the arrow pointing up to the right, you can press the right mouse button for a QuickMenu which offers options to select a sentence, paragraph, page, or the entire document.

Keyboard Steps

Use the arrow keys to position the cursor at the beginning of the text you want to select.

To select   **Press**

One character to the right .... `Shift` + `→`

One character to the left .... `Shift` + `←`

The line above .... `Shift` + `↑`

The line below .... `Shift` + `↓`

Text from the insertion
point to the end of the line .... `Shift` + `Alt`

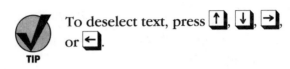

To deselect text, press ↑, ↓, →, or ←.

TIP

Exiting WordPerfect 6.0 for Windows

When you are ready to exit the program, click on the File menu and then click on the Exit command. WordPerfect will ask if you want to save your work, and you will then be returned safely to Windows.

Trademarks

All terms mentioned in this book that are known to be trademarks have been appropriately capitalized. Alpha Books cannot attest to the accuracy of this information. Use of a term in this book should not be regarded as affecting the validity of any trademark or service mark.

Abbreviations—Creating

Use the Abbreviations feature to quickly insert text you use frequently. First, give a short name (or abbreviation) to the frequently used text. Then whenever you want to use that text, you type in the abbreviation, and WordPerfect expands it to the full text. To use your abbreviations after you create them, see "Abbreviations—Expanding."

1. Select the text you
   want to abbreviate .... **F8**, ⬆ ⬇ ⬅ ➡

2. Open the Insert menu .... **Alt** + **I**

3. Choose **A**bbreviations .... **A**

4. Choose **C**reate .... **R**

5. Type a short abbreviation for the
   text, such as "busadd" for your
   business address .... ***text***

6. Choose **OK** .... ⬅

7. Close the Abbreviations
   dialog box .... **Alt** + **C**

Abbreviations—Expanding

Use this command to expand abbreviated text into the original version. To create an abbreviation, see "Abbreviations—Creating."

TIP

If you can't recall an abbreviation, place the cursor where you want the text, select Abbreviations from the Insert menu, and double-click on the abbreviation you want. WordPerfect inserts it at the cursor.

1. Enter the abbreviation where you want the full text to appear.

EXAMPLE

For example, type **busadd**.

2. Place the cursor anywhere on the abbreviation .... ↑ ↓ → ←

3. Open the Insert menu .... Alt + I

4. Choose **Abbreviations** .... A

5. Choose **Expand** .... Alt + E

TIP

You can also place the insertion point anywhere on the abbreviation and press **Ctrl+A** to expand it.

Blocks—Appending to the Clipboard

Use this command when you don't want to replace what is currently on the Clipboard, but you want to attach text to what is already there.

1. Select a block of text .... F8 , ↑ ↓ ← →

2. Open the Edit menu .... Alt + E

3. Choose **Append** .... D

Blocks—Centering

*Use this command to center a block of text. To right-
or left-justify text, see "Text—Justifying."*

Mouse Steps

1. Select a block of text.

2. Click the **Justification** button located on the
    Power Bar.

3. Drag to select **Center** and release the mouse
    button.

MOUSE

To center a single line, such as a heading,
click at the beginning of the line, click the
right mouse button, and select Center
from the QuickMenu.

Keyboard Steps

1. Select a block of text .... F8 , ↑ ↓ ← →

2. Open the Layout menu .... Alt + L

3. Choose Justification .... J

4. Select Center .... E

TIP

You can press **Ctrl+E** to center a selected
block of text instead of using the menus.

Blocks—Changing Case

Use this command to change a block of text to all lowercase, all uppercase, or first letter capitalized.

1. Select a block of text .... `F8`, `↑` `↓` `←` `→`

2. Open the Edit menu .... `Alt` + `E`

3. Select Convert Case .... `V`

4. Choose Lowercase, Uppercase, or Initial Capitals .... `L` or `U` or `I`

Blocks—Copying

Use this command to copy a block of text to a new location in a document. You can copy text to another document by opening that document before pasting. See "Document—Opening."

Mouse Steps

This is called "dragging and dropping."

1. Select a block of text.

2. Press and hold .... `Ctrl`

3. Place the mouse pointer on the selected text.

4. Press and hold the LEFT mouse button.

5. Drag to where you want the text copied.

6. Release the mouse button.

MOUSE

You can also copy text by using the **Copy** and **Paste** buttons located on the Power Bar, or by clicking the right mouse button and selecting the Copy and **Paste** commands from the QuickMenu.

Keyboard Steps

1. Select a block of text .... F8, ↑ ↓ ← →

2. Open the Edit menu .... Alt + E

3. Choose Copy C

4. Move the cursor to where you want the copied text to appear .... ↑ ↓ ← →

5. Open the Edit menu .... Alt + E

6. Choose Paste .... P

TIP

You can copy text by pressing **Ctrl+C** and paste text by pressing **Ctrl+V**.

Blocks—Deleting

Use this command to delete a block of text.

MOUSE

You can also delete text by selecting it, clicking the right mouse button, and selecting the **Delete** command.

1. Select a block of text .... F8, ↑ ↓ ← →
2. Press .... Delete or Back

Blocks—Moving

Use this command to move a block of text to a new location in the document. You can move text to another document by opening that document before pasting. See "Document—Opening."

Mouse Steps

This is called "dragging and dropping."

1. Select a block of text.

2. Place the mouse pointer on the selected text.

3. Press and hold the LEFT mouse button.

4. Drag to where you want the text moved.

5. Release the mouse button.

MOUSE

You can also move text by using the **Cut** and **Paste** buttons located on the Power Bar, or by clicking the right mouse button and selecting the **C**ut and **P**aste commands from the QuickMenu.

Keyboard Steps

1. Select a block of text .... F8, ↑ ↓ ← →
2. Open the **E**dit menu .... Alt + E
3. Choose Cut .... T

4. Move the cursor to where you want the text moved ....

5. Select the Edit menu .... **Alt** + **E**

6. Choose **Paste** .... **P**

> You can cut text by pressing **Ctrl+X** and paste text by pressing **Ctrl+V**.
>
> **TIP**

Blocks—Printing

Use this command to print a block of text. For information on printing pages, see "Page—Printing."

1. Select a block of text **F8**,

2. Open the File menu .... **Alt** + **F**

3. Select **Print** .... **P**

> You can press **F5** to access the Print dialog box instead of following steps 2 and 3.
>
> **TIP**

> Instead of steps 2 and 3, click on the **Print** button on the Power Bar.
>
> **MOUSE**

4. Select Enter. ....

Blocks—Protecting from Page Split

Use this command to prevent a block of text from being split over two pages.

TIP

If you later add or delete text in the block, the new text will be protected, too. Be sure to add any new text within the block.

1. Select a block of text ....`F8`, `↑` `↓` `←` `→`

2. Open the Layout menu ....`Alt` + `L`

3. Choose **Page** ....`P`

4. Choose **Keep** Text Together ....`K`

MOUSE

Instead of steps 2 and 3, click on the **Keep Text Together** button on the Page Button Bar.

5. Choose **Keep** selected text together on same page ....`K`

6. Choose OK ....`⏎`

Blocks—Saving

Use this command to save a block of text in its own file.

1. Select a block of text ....`F8`, `↑` `↓` `←` `→`

2. Open the File menu .... Alt + F

3. Select Save .... S

> You can press **Ctrl+S** to access the File
> Save dialog box, instead of following steps
> 2 and 3.
>
> **TIP**

> Instead of steps 2 and 3, click on the **Save**
> button on the Power Bar.
>
> **MOUSE**

4. Select **OK** .... ⏎

5. **(Optional)** To change drives,
   press .... Alt + V
   and select a drive letter .... ↑ ↓ ← →

6. **(Optional)** To change directories,
   press .... Alt + D
   and select a directory .... ↑ ↓ ← →

7. **(Optional)** If necessary, move to
   the Filename list .... Alt + N

8. Type the file name
   in which to save the block .... *filename.ext*

9. Select **OK** .... ⏎

Blocks—Selecting

Use this command to select a block of text.

Mouse Steps

1. Click on the first character in the block.

2. Press **Shift**.

3. Click after the last character in the block.

MOUSE   You can also drag over characters to select them, or drag within the selection bar at the left margin.

MOUSE   To quickly select words, sentences, or paragraphs, click with the right mouse button in the left margin and select the appropriate command from the QuickMenu, or:

You can also	*to select*
Double-click	a word
Triple-click	a sentence
Quadruple-click	a paragraph

4. Perform any block command.

TIP   To cancel a selection, click anywhere in the document.

Keyboard Steps

1. Move to the first character
   in the block .... ⬆️ ⬇️ ⬅️ ➡️

2. Change to Block mode F8

3. Move to the last character
   in the block .... ⬆️ ⬇️ ⬅️ ➡️

   Or, after changing to Block mode:

You can press	To select
⬆️	One line up
⬇️	One line down
Shift+End	To the end of the line
Shift+Home	To the beginning of a line
Shift+Ctrl+➡️ or ⬅️	One word at a time
Shift+Ctrl+⬆️	One paragraph up
Shift+Ctrl+⬇️	One paragraph down
Shift+Ctrl+Home	To the beginning of a document
Shift+Ctrl+End	To the end of a document

4. Perform any block command.

TIP

To cancel the block selection, press **F8** again.

Bookmarks—Creating

A bookmark is an invisible marker that allows you to move quickly between locations in your document. See also "Bookmarks—Finding" and "Bookmarks—Deleting." You can highlight text before setting a bookmark, and later return to the bookmark and have the text already selected for you. See "Bookmarks—Finding."

For example, if you are writing a long article, you may need to move back and forth to check references and relocate text.

Use this command to create a bookmark.

1. Position the cursor where you want the bookmark .... ⬆ ⬇ ⬅ ➡

2. Open the Insert menu .... **Alt** + **I**

3. Select **B**ookmark .... **B**

4. Select Cr**e**ate .... **Alt** + **E**

5. Type the **B**ookmark name in the text box .... *name*

6. Select **OK** .... ⏎

Bookmark names are case-sensitive: a bookmark that is called *TIPS* is different from a bookmark called *tips*.

Bookmarks—Creating a QuickMark

If you need only one bookmark in your document, you can create a QuickMark. It has no name, and you select it as often as you want with only a few keystrokes. Use this command to create a QuickMark.

1. Position the cursor where you want the QuickMark.................. ⬆ ⬇ ⬅ ➡

2. Open the Insert menu .... Alt + I

3. Select **B**ookmark .... B

4. Select Set **Q**uickMark...................... Alt + Q

Instead of using the menu, you can press **Ctrl+Shift+Q** to set a QuickMark.

TIP

Later, to find the QuickMark in your document, open the Insert menu and select **B**ookmark. Then choose Find QuickMark.

TIP

Bookmarks—Deleting

Use this command to delete a bookmark.

1. Select the Insert menu .... Alt + I

2. Select **B**ookmark .... B

3. Highlight the bookmark you want
   to delete .... ⇧⤒ ⇩

4. Select **Delete** .... **Alt** + **D**

5. Select **Yes** .... **Y**

6. Select **Close** .... **Alt** + **C** or **Esc**

Bookmarks—Finding

*Use this command to find a bookmark that you
have created.*

1. Open the **Insert** menu .... **Alt** + **I**

2. Select **Bookmark** .... **B**

3. Select the name of the bookmark
   you want to find .... ⤒ ⇩

4. Select **Go** To to move to the
   bookmark .... **Alt** + **G**

MOUSE

If you highlighted the bookmark when you
created it, the word "Selected" appears
under Type in the Bookmark dialog box.
You can automatically select the bookmark
text as you go to it. Simply click on Go To
& Select, or press **Alt+S** at step 4.

Bullet List—Creating

*Use this command to change text into a bulleted list
of items.*

1. **(Optional)** Select the text
   you want to convert to a list .. **F8**, ⤒ ⇩ ⬅ ➡

2. Choose the Insert menu .... Alt + I

3. Select Bullets & Numbers .... N

MOUSE

Instead of steps 2 and 3, click on the **Bullets & Numbers** button on the WordPerfect Button Bar.

4. Select a style of bullets from the Styles list .... ↑ ↓

5. Select OK .... ↵

TIP

Instead of using the menus, you can press **Ctrl+Shift+B** to insert a bullet (in a previously selected style) at the cursor position.

TIP

When you want to create a bulleted list from the beginning, follow the same steps without selecting text. Just enter the bullet list commands and, before step 5, select New Bullet or Number on Enter by clicking on it or pressing **N**. To resume normal typing, follow these steps to access the Bullets and Numbers dialog box, and deselect New Bullet or Number on Enter by clicking on it or pressing **N** again.

Button Bars—Selecting

WordPerfect comes with twelve Button Bars you can use for speedy access to groups of related features. Button Bars can be used only with the mouse, but you can select one for display with the keyboard. The available Button Bars are Equation Editor, Font, Generate, Graphics, Layout, Macros, Outline, Page, Preferences, Tables, WordPerfect, and WordPerfect 5.2. Use these steps to select a Button Bar for display.

Mouse Steps

1. With the RIGHT mouse button, click anywhere on the currently displayed Button Bar.

2. Select a Button Bar from the QuickMenu.

Keyboard Steps

1. Open the File menu .... `Alt` + `F`

2. Select Preferences .... `E`

3. Select Button Bar .... `Alt` + `B`

4. Press .... `⏎`

5. Select a Button Bar
   from the list .... `↑` `↓` `←` `→`

6. Choose Select .... `Alt` + `S`

7. Select Close .... `Alt` + `C`

Codes—Deleting

Use this command to delete a hidden text code, such as a hard return or margin settings.

1. Open the View menu .... `Alt` + `V`

2. Select Reveal Codes .... `C`

TIP

You can press **Alt+F3** instead of following steps 1 and 2.

3. Click on the hidden code you want to delete, or move the cursor in front of the hidden code .... ⬆ ⬇ ⬅ ➡

4. Press .... Delete

Codes—Revealing and Hiding

Use this command to reveal or hide the text codes that provide instructions to WordPerfect, such as codes telling where to begin and end the following formatting and style features:

- Bold, underline, italic, or other text enhancement

- Margin settings

- Page numbering

- Indents, tabs, and columns

- Hard and soft returns

TIP

Use the same steps to reveal and hide codes. Like a light switch in your home, perform the steps to turn the option on and repeat them to turn it off. This is called a toggle.

When hidden codes are deleted, affected text re-
turns to normal. To see codes revealed or hidden:

1. Choose the **View** menu .... Alt + V
2. Select Reveal Codes C

TIP

You can press **Alt+F3** instead of following steps 1 and 2.

MOUSE

To turn off Reveal Codes quickly, click the right mouse button within the Reveal Codes window. Click on **H**ide Reveal Codes from the QuickMenu.

Columns

WordPerfect lets you create four kinds of columns
from your text:

Newspaper style	Text flows from the bottom of one column to the top of the next, like a newspaper. See "Columns—Creating Newspaper Columns."
Balanced News-paper style	Text flows like newspaper columns except that each column is adjusted on the page so they are equal in length. See "Columns— Creating Newspaper Col-umns."

Parallel style	Individual items have their own columns, like a table. For example, a resume or a list like this one uses parallel columns. See "Columns—Creating Parallel Columns."
Parallel style with Block Protect	This style keeps each row of columns together on the same page. See "Columns—Creating Parallel Columns."

To turn off columns and return to normal text, see "Columns—Turning Off."

Columns—Creating Newspaper Columns

There are two types of newspaper-style columns from which to choose. With Newspaper, the text columns are uneven. With Balanced Newspaper, the text in each column is adjusted so that the columns are even along their bottom edges.

Mouse Steps

1. Move to where you want the columns to begin.

2. Click the **Columns Define** button located on the Power Bar.

3. Drag to the number of columns desired and release the mouse button.

To create Balanced Newspaper style columns, select Define at step 3. Then select **B**alanced Newspaper under Type.

TIP

Keyboard Steps

1. Move to where you want the columns to begin .... ⬆ ⬇ ⬅ ➡

2. Select the Layout menu .... **Alt** + **L**

3. Choose Columns .... **C**

4. Choose **D**efine .... **D**

5. Type the number of columns desired .... *number*

6. Select **N**ewspaper or **B**alanced Newspaper .... **Alt** + **N** or **B**

7. Select **OK** .... ⏎

You can make columns from regular text you have already typed. Just select the text you want in columns and then follow the steps for creating columns.

TIP

Columns—Creating Parallel Columns

There are two types of parallel-style columns from which to choose. With Parallel, one column can extend to the next page, regardless of the lengths of the other columns. With Parallel w/ Block Protect, if one column extends to the next page, the horizontal block of text is moved to the next page.

TIP

Rather than creating parallel style columns, you can create a table with a grid for entering and displaying data. See "Tables—Creating."

Mouse Steps

1. Move the cursor to where you want the columns to begin.

2. Click the **Columns Define** button located on the Power Bar.

3. Select Define.

4. Enter the desired number of columns

5. Click on **P**arallel or **P**arallel w/ Block Protect.

6. Click on **OK**.

Keyboard Steps

1. Move to where you want the columns to begin .... ↑ ↓ → ←

2. Select the Layout menu .... **Alt** + **L**

3. Choose Columns .... **C**

4. Choose Define .... **D**

5. Enter the number of columns you want in the text box .... *number*

6. Choose **P**arallel or **P**arallel w/
   BlockProtect .... Alt + P or A

7. Select **OK** .... Tab or ↑ ↓ ← →
                                              ↵

Columns—Entering Text

Use this command to enter text into parallel columns. (To enter text into newspaper-style columns, just type! When you reach the end of a column, WordPerfect will automatically move the cursor to the top of the next column.)

1. Enter text into the first column ....**text**

2. Move to the next parallel
   column .... Ctrl + ↵

Columns—Moving Within and Between

Use these commands to move around and between columns.

Mouse Steps

Click within a column to move the insertion point.

Keyboard Steps

To move...	Press...
One character to the left or right	← or →
One line up or down within a column	↑ or ↓

To move...	Press...
Next column in same row	Alt + →
Previous column in same row	Alt + ←
Top of current column on this screen	Alt + Home
Bottom of current column on this screen	Alt + End

Columns—Turning Off

Use this command to turn off columns and return to normal margins within your document.

Mouse Steps

1. Move past the last character in the last column.

2. Click the **Columns Define** button located on the Power Bar.

3. Select Columns Off.

Keyboard Steps

1. Move past the last character in the last column.

2. Open the Layout menu .... Alt + L

3. Choose Columns C

4. Choose Off .... O

TIP

To change column text into regular text, either delete the column definition code (see "Codes—Deleting") or move to the beginning of the column and follow these instructions to turn columns off.

Commands—Cancelling

Use this procedure to cancel the last command you entered.

1. Select the **E**dit menu ....**Alt** + **E**

2. Select **U**ndo ....**U**

TIP

To undo your last command even faster, press **Ctrl+Z**.

MOUSE

Instead of steps 1 and 2, click on the **Undo** button located on the Power Bar.

Comments—Changing Comment into Text

A comment contains information that you want to keep track of, but not add to the printed document. For example, you could use comments to add personal notes that are not printed. Comments are displayed on-screen with a balloon icon in the margin. Use this command to change a comment into regular text that prints with the rest of the document. To create a comment, see "Comments—Creating." To change existing text into a comment,

see "Comments—Changing Text into a Comment."
To read a comment, see "Comments—Revealing."

1. Place the cursor just after the comment.
2. Open the Insert menu.
3. Choose Comment.
4. Choose Convert to Text.

Comments—Changing Text into a Comment

Use this command to change existing text into a comment.

1. Select the text you want to convert to a comment.
2. Open the Insert menu.
3. Select Comment.
4. Select Create.

Comments—Creating

Use this command to add non-printing notes and other comments to your documents.

1. Open the Insert menu.
2. Choose Comment.
3. Choose Create.
4. Enter your comment ....***text***
5. Select Close.

TIP

You can print a comment if you convert it to text. See "Comments—Changing Comment into Text."

MOUSE

If you want to insert your initials or name, the date, or the current time, click the appropriate button on the Comments Feature Bar.

Comments—Deleting

Use this command to delete an unwanted comment.

1. Turn on Reveal Codes ....`Alt` + `F3`

2. Click on the comment code.

3. Press ....`Delete`

4. Turn off Reveal Codes ....`Alt` + `F3`

Comments—Editing

You cannot edit comments as if they were regular text; the cursor refuses to move into a comment. Use this command to edit your comments.

1. Turn on Reveal Codes ....`Alt` + `F3`

2. Double-click on the comment code.

3. Make changes to the comment as needed.

4. Choose Close.

5. Turn off Reveal Codes ....`Alt` + `F3`

Comments—Revealing

Use this command to display the contents of a comment.

Click on the balloon icon in the left margin.

Cross-References—Creating

Use this command to create cross-references in your document. You can cross-reference page numbers, sections, footnotes, endnotes, and graphics with this feature. The reference code marks the location in the document where the reference appears; the target code marks the item you want to reference.

EXAMPLE If on page 15 you want to refer to information on page 32, place the reference code on page 15, and the target code on page 32. Your reference reads "For more information, refer to page 32."

1. Place the cursor in the text where you want areference code.

2. Type the reference with a space at the end ....*reference*

EXAMPLE For example, type: **For more information, refer to the chart on page** .

3. Click the Cross-Ref button on the Generate Button Bar.

4. Click the **R**eference button.

5. Click on a reference type.

6. Type a target name in the ....*targetname* **T**arget box.

EXAMPLE   For example, type **Table 1A**.

7. Click on Mark **R**eference.

8. Click at the beginning of the target text.

9. Click on Mark **T**arget.

10. Click **G**enerate.

11. Click **C**lose.

Data File—Creating

A data file is used as part of a merge operation; see "Document—Merging Data and Form Files" for more information. Use this command to create a file containing the sets of data that will be merged into the form file.

1. Click the **New** button on the Power Bar.

2. Click on the **Merge** button on the WordPerfect Button Bar.

3. To create a data file, click on **P**lace Records in a Table.

4. Click on **Data**.

5. Type the name of a field ....*field name*

EXAMPLE

For example, First_Name, Last_Name, Address1, and so on.

6. Click on **Add**.

7. Repeat steps 5 and 6 for each field.

8. Click on OK.

9. Enter the data for the first field.

10. Move to the next field or record and enter data.

11. Repeat steps 9 and 10 for each field and record.

12. Click on **Close**.

13. Click on **Yes** to save the data file.

14. Type in a filename.

15. Click on **OK**.

TIP

For information on creating form files, see "Form File—Creating."

Date and Time—Inserting

Use this command to insert the current date and/or time into a document. You can insert either the current date and/or time as text or a code that WordPerfect updates to the current date and time each time you retrieve the document.

TIP

By default, WordPerfect inserts a date in the format **October 16, 1993**. To insert the time, the date and time together, or to use a different date format (such as 10/16/93), see "Date and Time—Setting the Format."

Mouse Steps

1. Place the cursor where you want to insert the date, the time, or both.

2. Click on the **Date Text** button on the WordPerfect Button Bar.

TIP

To insert the date as a code, use the Insert Date command described next.

Keyboard Steps

1. Move the cursor to where you want the date and/or time....⬆ ⬇ ⬅ ➡

2. Open the Insert menu......................Alt + I

3. Select Date..D

4. Choose Date **T**ext or Date **C**ode .... T or C

TIP

To insert a date quickly with the keyboard, press **Ctrl+D** to insert date text, and **Ctrl+Shift+D** to insert date code.

Date and Time—Setting the Format

Use this command to control the format WordPerfect uses when it enters date and time into your document.

TIP

Changing the date format will affect all date codes inserted after you use this command.

1. Place the cursor before the date code you want to affect .... ↑ ↓ ← →

2. Open the Insert menu .... Alt + I

3. Select **D**ate .... D

4. Select Date **F**ormat .... F

5. Select a date format from the Predefined Formats list .... ↑ ↓ ← →

6. Select **OK** .... ↵

Document—Closing

Use this command to close a document.

1. Open the **F**ile menu .... Alt + F

2. Choose Close C

Instead of steps 1 and 2, press **Ctrl+F4**.

TIP

Instead of steps 1 and 2, double-click on the document window's Control-menu box.

MOUSE

3. Choose whether to save the document .... Y or N

4. If you chose Y and the document has not been saved before, type a name for the document .... *filename.ext*

5. (Optional) If necessary, use the Drives list box to change to a different drive .... Alt + V
   ↑ or ↓

6. (Optional) If necessary, use the Directories list box to select another directory .... Alt + D
   ↑ or ↓

7. Select **OK** .... ↵

Document—Comparing

Use this command to compare a new version of a document with an old one. In the new document, additions will be marked with redline, and dele-tions will be marked with strikeout formatting.

EXAMPLE If you wrote a report for your boss and she sent you a revised version, you could compare it to your original to see what she changed.

TIP Make sure you have opened the newest version of the document you want to compare. See "Document—Opening."

1. Select the File menu .... Alt + F

2. Choose Compare Document .... R

3. Select Add Markings .... A

4. **(Optional)** Enter the name of the original document in the Compare Current Document to list box ....*filename.ext*

MOUSE Click on the file icon to locate a file.

5. Select how you want to compare: by Word, Phrase, Sentence, or Paragraph..................... W or R
   or S or P

6. Select OK... ⏎

Document—Line Spacing

Use this command to change the line spacing (single, double, or triple space) in your document.

1. Select the Layout menu .... Alt + L

2. Choose Line L

3. Choose Spacing .... S

4. Enter the amount of line spacing
   you desire .... *number*

5. Select OK .... ⏎

You can vary the line spacing within your document by repeating these steps at any later time.

TIP

Document—Locking

Use this command to add a password when saving a file so as to prevent unauthorized access.

Write the password down! You must remember it to access this document later on.

TIP

1. Open the File menu .... Alt + F

2. Select Save As .... A

Instead of following steps 1 and 2, press **F3**.

3. Choose **P**assword Protect ....**Alt** + **P**

4. Choose **OK** ....**↵**

5. Enter the password (up to 23 characters) ....*password*

6. Choose **OK** ....**↵**

7. Repeat the password to confirm it ....*password*

8. Choose **OK** ....**↵**

Document—Merging Data and Form Files

Use this command to merge a data file with a form file. To create a data file, see "Data File—Creating." To create a form file, see "Form File—Creating."

EXAMPLE To create a form business letter, merge a form file containing the letter text with a date file containing names and addresses to be entered in the heading where the data fields are referenced.

TIP Before you merge your data file with your form letter or envelope file, you can sort the data file first. See "Document—Sorting Data Files."

1. Select the **Merge** button from the Merge Feature Bar.

2. Select **Merge**.

3. **(Optional)** If necessary, enter the names of the **F**orm File.

4. **(Optional)** If necessary, enter the names of the **D**ata File.

5. Enter the name of the Output File.

6. Click **OK**.

TIP You can select specific records to merge or merge to create envelopes. See "Document—Merging Selected Records" or "Document—Merging to Envelopes."

Document—Merging Selected Records

Use this command from within the Perform Merge dialog box to select data file records for your merge with the form file. See "Document—Merging Data and Form Files."

1. From within the Perform Merge dialog box, choose **S**elect Records.

2. Select either **S**pecifying Conditions or **M**ark Records.

3. If you chose **S**pecifying Conditions, select a **F**ield and enter a condition. (If you chose Mark Records, skip to step 5.)

Condition	Example	What it selects
value	Smith	People named Smith
value1, value2	Jones, Smith	People named Jones or Smith
fromvalue– tovalue	Johnson-Jones	People whose names are between Johnson and Jones
![*notvalue*]	![Smith]	Everyone *not* named Smith

4. **(Optional)** Instead of steps 2 and 4 specify a Record Number Range and skip to step 8.

5. If you chose **Mark Records**, select the records you wish to merge from the Record List by clicking on them.

TIP

If you need to mark all records except a few, select **Mark all Records** and then unmark the specific ones you don't need.

6. **(Optional)** Select which records to display in the list by entering a beginning and ending record number.

7. **(Optional)** Choose the **First Field to Display** in the list.

8. Click **OK**.

Document—Merging to Envelopes

Use this command from within the Perform Merge dialog box to create multiple envelopes with your data file. See "Document—Merging Data and Form Files."

1. From the Perform Merge dialog box, select Envelopes.

2. If necessary, enter the Return Address.

MOUSE

If you don't want to print a return address, click on Print Return Address to deselect it.

3. **(Optional)** Select the return address and change its font.

4. **(Optional)** Select Add to save the return address for future use.

TIP

Instead of steps 2 through 4, select a saved address from the return address list.

5. Click within the Mailing Addresses box.

6. Insert a field.

7. Insert necessary punctuation.

8. Repeat steps 6 and 7 for each field in the address.

9. Select an envelope definition or create your own.

10. Click **OK**.

11. Click **OK** again.

12. Print your envelopes by clicking the **Print** button on the Power Bar.

13. Save your envelope file by clicking the **Save** button on the Power Bar.

Document—Moving Within

Use these commands to move within your document with the keyboard or the mouse.

Mouse Movements

To move...	Click here...
Down one line	Down arrow of the vertical scroll bar.
Up one line	Up arrow of the vertical scroll bar.
Next page	Next Page button of the vertical scroll bar.
Previous page	Previous Page button of the vertical scroll bar.
One character right	Right arrow of the horizontal scroll bar.
One character left	Left arrow of the horizontal scroll bar.
One screen down	Between the arrows on the vertical scroll bar.

Keyboard Movements

To move...	Use...
Left or right one character	← or →
Left or right one word	Ctrl + ← or Ctrl + →
Up or down one paragraph	Ctrl + ↑ or Ctrl + ↓
Beginning of a line	Home
End of a line	End
Up or down one line	↑ or ↓
Up or down one page	Page Up or Page Down
To a specific page	Ctrl + G Alt + N page number ↵
Between columns	Alt + → or Alt + ←
To a specific position in the document	Ctrl + G Alt + P ↑ or ↓ ↵
Beginning of document	Ctrl + Home
End of document	Ctrl + End

Document—Opening

Use this procedure to open a document in a new window.

1. Select the File menu .... Alt + F

2. Select Open .... O

TIP

Instead of steps 1 and 2, press **Ctrl+O** or **F4**.

MOUSE

Instead of steps 1 and 2, click on the **Open** button on the Power Bar.

3. Type the document name or
   select it .... *filename.ext*
   or ↑ ↓

4. **(Optional)** Change drives .... Alt + V
   ↓

5. **(Optional)** Change directories .... Alt + D
   ↓

6. Select **OK** .... ↵

Document—Printing

Use this command to print an open document.

TIP

You can also print a document without opening it. Select the **File Open** command, choose File **Options**, and then select **Print**. Select the file you want to print and select the **Print** button. You can select several files and print them all at once if you like: see "Files—Marking."

1. **(Optional)** Select text to print.

2. Open the File menu .... `Alt` + `F`

3. Choose **Print** .... `P`

> **MOUSE**
>
> Instead of steps 2 and 3, click on the **Print** button on the Power Bar.

4. **(Optional)** If you don't want to print the entire document, choose from these options:

   Selected Text: Prints only
   selected text .... `L`

   Current Page: Prints just
   the current page .... `U`

   Multiple Pages: Prints the
   pages you specify .... `M`

> **TIP**
>
> If you choose Multiple Pages, after selecting **Print**, you will see a dialog box asking you to specify page numbers. Enter pages like this: **2** or **2,4** or **2–6,10**.

   Document Summary: Prints
   just the summary .... `A`

   Document on Disk: Saves the
   print image to a file on disk
   for printing on another PC .... `D`

5. **(Optional)** Choose Number of
   Copies. Then type the number of
   copies desired .... N
   number

6. **(Optional)** Choose whether to have
   the printer generate extra copies .... Alt + E
   ↑ ↓

7. **(Optional)** Change the print
   Quality .... Alt + Q

> For example, to save time printing the first
> draft of a report, select **Draft** quality.
>
> **EXAMPLE**

8. **(Optional)** Select a Print Color ...... Alt + R

9. **(Optional)** To save time on a draft
   copy, select Do not Print Graphics .. Alt + G

10. Choose **Print** .... Alt + P

Document—Renaming and Relocating

*Use this command to save an existing document
under a new name, or in a new drive or directory.*

When you perform these steps, you will
have two copies of the document—one file
under the old name (or in the old location) and one file under the new name or
location.

TIP

1. Open the File menu .... Alt + F

2. Select Save As .... A

TIP

Instead of steps 1 and 2, press **F3**.

3. Type in the new name of your
   document in the dialog box .... *filename.ext*

4. **(Optional)** Select Drives and
   choose a new drive .... Alt + V
   ↑ ↓

5. **(Optional)** Select Directories and
   choose a different directory .... Alt + D
   ↑ ↓

6. Select **OK** .... ↵

7. If prompted, choose whether to
   replace the existing file .... Y or N

8. If you do not replace it, enter a
   different name .... *filename.ext*

9. Select **OK** .... ↵

Document—Saving

Use this command to save a document.

1. Open the File menu .... Alt + F

2. Select Save .... S

TIP

Instead of steps 1 and 2, press **Ctrl+S**.

MOUSE

Instead of steps 1 and 2, click on the **Save** button on the Power Bar.

3. If the document has not been saved previously, type a name ....*filename.ext*

4. Select **OK**..⏎

Document—Saving Automatically

Use this command to save your documents auto-matically at specified timed intervals.

Mouse Steps

1. Select the File menu ....Alt + F

2. Choose Preferences ....E

3. Choose File ....Alt + F
⏎

MOUSE

Instead of steps 1 to 3, click on the **Files** button on the Preferences Button Bar.

4. Select a backup time interval in the
   Timed Document Backup every
   ___ minutes box ....`Alt` + `C`
                       # or `↑` `↓`

5. Choose **OK** ....`⏎`

6. Select Close ....`Alt` + `C`

Document—Search Results

*Use this command to work with the results of a
search using QuickFinder.*

To select multiple files, see
"Files—Marking."

TIP

1. Select a file from the list.

2. Choose an option:

   Open—Opens the selected files ......`Alt` + `N`

   View—Opens files for viewing
   only ....`Alt` + `W`

   File Options ....`Alt` + `O`+*letter below*

   Copy—Makes a copy of
   selected files ....`C`

   Move—Moves selected files to a
   different drive or directory.......................`M`

   Rename—Renames selected files ....`R`

Delete—Deletes selected files .... D

Change Attributes—Changes files'
attributes .... A

Print—Prints selected files .... P

Print List—Prints all files or the
selected files L

Sort Setup—Changes the order of
displayed files .... Alt + S

By .... B

Order .... O + ↑ ↓

↵

3. Select Close .... Alt + C

Document—Searching For

*To locate a document, see either "QuickFinder—
Using" (to locate a file based on its contents or the
date it was created or changed) or "QuickList—
Using" (to build a list of often used files).*

Document—Sorting Data Files

*Use this command to sort a data file prior to a
merge.*

1. **(Optional)** If necessary, click on **G**o to Data
   on the Merge Feature Bar.

2. Click the **O**ptions button on the Merge Data
   File Feature Bar.

3. Select **S**ort.

4. **(Optional)** If necessary, enter the name of the data file to sort under **I**nput File.

5. **(Optional)** If you want, enter a name for the new sorted data file.

6. Select a sort option: **L**ine, **P**aragraph, **T**able Row, **M**erge Record, or **C**olumn.

7. Select a sort key.
   If necessary, change the sort type.
   Choose either ascending or descending order.
   Choose to sort by Field, Line, or Word.
   Enter the field, line, or word number to sort by.

8. **(Optional)** Add a new sort key.

9. Select **OK**.

Document—Sorting Text Within

Use this command to sort a document. Documents can be sorted by line (such as an employee list) or paragraph (such as a dictionary or a legal contract). Lines end with a hard or soft return, and paragraphs end with two hard returns. Data merge documents can also be sorted: see "Document—Sorting Data Files."

EXAMPLE

You could first sort an employee list by last name (key 1) and then by first name (key 2), or "first name within last name."

1. Select the Tools menu .... `Alt` + `T`
2. Choose Sort .... `R`

> **TIP**
>
> Instead of steps 1 and 2, press **Alt+F9**.

3. **(Optional)** Choose Input File .... `I`
   Then type the name of the
   document to sort ....*filename.ext*
   `↵`

4. **(Optional)** Choose Output File ...... `Alt` + `O`
   Then type the name of the output
   document ....*filename.ext*

5. Choose Line or **Paragraph** .... `Alt` + `L`
   or `Alt` + `P`

6. **(Optional)** Set up the desired sort keys:
   Select the key .... `Alt` + *key number*
   Choose a sort type .... `Tab` + `↑` `↓`
   Choose a sort order .... `Tab` + `↑` `↓`
   Choose which Field, Line,
   or Word to sort on................ `Tab` + *number*

7. **(Optional)** Select a key option:
   Add a key .... `Alt` + `A`
   Delete the highlighted key .... `Alt` + `D`
   Insert a key before the highlighted
   one .... `Alt` + `I`

8. **(Optional)** Repeat steps 6 and 7 for additional sort keys.

9. Select **OK** .... ⏎

Document Information— Accessing

Use this command to get information about the document, such as the number of words and the date last edited.

1. Select the **F**ile menu .... `Alt` + `F`

2. Choose Document **I**nfo .... `I`

3. After reviewing the information, choose **OK** .... ⏎

Drag and Drop—Text Editing

This term refers to using your mouse to cut, copy, and paste information. See "Blocks—Copying" and "Blocks—Moving."

Envelope—Creating

Use this command to address and print an envelope.

1. Select the **L**ayout menu .... `Alt` + `L`

2. Select En**v**elope .... `V`

Instead of steps 1 and 2, click on the **Envelope** button on the WordPerfect Button Bar.

3. Select a return address from
   the list, or type the return address
   text in its box ....`Alt` + `R`
   `↑` `↓` or *address text*

4. (**Optional**) Add the return
   address ....`Alt` + `A`

> **TIP**
>
> To not print a return address, click Print
> Return Address to deselect it. Also, change
> the font of the return address by clicking
> on Font. See "Fonts—Changing."

5. Type the mailing address
   text in its box, or select one
   from the list ....`Alt` + `M`
   `↑` `↓` or *address text*

6. Select the envelope size from
   the Envelope Definitions box..........`Alt` + `V`
   `↑` `↓`

7. (**Optional**) Create a New Definition
   and enter the dimensions of the
   envelope ....`Alt` + `W`
   sizes

8. Select Print Envelope or
   Append To Doc..........................`Alt` + `P` or
   `Alt` + `T`

Exiting WordPerfect for Windows

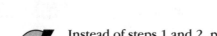

Use this command to exit WordPerfect.

1. Open the File menu ....<kbd>Alt</kbd> + <kbd>F</kbd>
2. Select Exit ....<kbd>X</kbd>

Instead of steps 1 and 2, press **Alt+F4**.

TIP

Instead of following steps 1 and 2, double-click on the program's Control-menu box.

MOUSE

3. **(Optional)** Save any document changes by clicking on **Yes** ....<kbd>Y</kbd>
4. **(Optional)** If a document has not yet been saved, enter a file name ....***filename.ext***
5. Select **OK**...<kbd>←</kbd>

Faxing

Use this command along with your fax software to prepare a document for faxing through your PC's modem.

1. Open the File menu ....<kbd>Alt</kbd> + <kbd>F</kbd>
2. Choose Select Printer ....<kbd>L</kbd>
3. Select your fax port ....<kbd>↑</kbd><kbd>↓</kbd>

4. Choose Close .... $\boxed{\text{Alt}}$ + $\boxed{\text{C}}$
5. Print the document .... $\boxed{\text{F5}}$

Instead of step 5, click on the **Print** button on the Power Bar.

MOUSE

6. Complete the necessary information for your fax program.

Feature Bars—Accessing with the Keyboard

Feature bars appear when you are performing certain complex commands, such as adding foot-notes or working with graphics. Use this command to access a feature bar with the keyboard.

1. Press... $\boxed{\text{Alt}}$ + $\boxed{\text{Shift}}$
2. Press the underlined letter of the feature bar button you want to access ....*underlined letter*

Files—Copying

Use this command to copy a file to a different directory or drive. You can even change the file name as you copy the file if you want.

To select multiple files for copying, see "Files—Marking."

TIP

TIP

You can copy a file without opening it.

1. Select File .... Alt + F

2. Select Open .... O

TIP

Instead of steps 1 and 2, press **Ctrl+O**.

MOUSE

Instead of steps 1 and 2, click on the **Open** button on the Power Bar.

3. Choose the file you want to copy .... ↑ ↓

4. Select File Options .... Alt + O

5. Choose Copy C

6. Type the new drive directory, or filename .... ***drive:\directory\filename***

EXAMPLE

To change the name of the copied file, type it after the drive and directory, as in C:\WORK\NEW.DOC.

7. Select Copy .... ↵

Files—Deleting

Use this command to delete a file from disk.

TIP

To select multiple files for deleting, see "Files—Marking."

1. Select File ....Alt + F
2. Select Open ....O

TIP

Instead of steps 1 and 2, press **Ctrl+O**.

MOUSE

Instead of steps 1 and 2, click on the **Open** button on the Power Bar.

3. Choose the file you want to delete ....↑ ↓
4. Select File Options ....Alt + O
5. Choose Delete ....D
6. Select Delete again. ....↵

Files—Marking

Use this command to mark multiple files within a file selection box.

Mouse Steps

1. Click on the first file.

2. **(Optional)** To select contiguous files, press **Shift** and click on the last file.

3. **(Optional)** To select non-contiguous files, press **Ctrl** and click on each file.

Keyboard Steps

1. Move to the first file .... ⬆ ⬇

2. **(Optional)** To select contiguous files, press .... Shift
   and move to the last file .... ⬆ ⬇

3. **(Optional)** To select non-contiguous files, press .... Shift + F8
   and select each file .... Space

Files—Moving or Renaming

Use this command to move or rename a file from disk.

TIP

To select multiple files for moving or renaming, see "Files—Marking."

1. Select **File** .... Alt + F

2. Select **Open** .... O

Instead of steps 1 and 2, press **Ctrl+O**.

TIP

Instead of steps 1 and 2, click on the
Open button on the Power Bar.

MOUSE

3. Choose the file you want to move
   or rename .... ↑ ↓

4. Select File Options .... Alt + O

5. Choose **Move** or **Rename** .... M or R

6. If you are moving a file, type
   the new drive or directory for
   the file .... *drive:\directory*
   If you are renaming a file, type
   in the new name for the file .... *filename.ext*

7. Select **Move** or **Rename** again. .... M or R

Fonts—Changing

*Use this command to change the appearance of
your text, by the letter, by the word, or by a large
block.*

You can copy the formatting of text in one
easy step. See "QuickFormat—Using."

TIP

Mouse Steps

1. **(Optional)** Select the text you want to format.

TIP You can select text and then change its font, or you can follow these steps to change the font as you type. If you change the appearance of text as you type, remember to change the text settings back to normal at the appropriate point.

2. Click the **Font Face** button on the Power Bar.

3. Select a font.

4. **(Optional)** Change the point size by clicking the **Font Size** button on the Power Bar.

5. **(Optional)** Change the appearance of text with the appropriate buttons on the Font Button Bar:

    Bold

    Underline

    Double Underline

    Italics

    Outline

    Shadow

    Small Caps

    Redline

    Strikeout

MOUSE

Bold, italics, and underline buttons can also be found on the Power Bar. In addition, you can change many attributes at once by clicking the **Font** button on the Font Button Bar.

Keyboard Steps

1. **(Optional)** Select the text you want to format .... F8, ↑ ↓ ← →

TIP

You can select text and then change its font, or you can follow these steps to change the font as you type. If you change the appearance of text as you type, remember to change the text settings back to normal at the appropriate point.

2. Open the Layout menu .... Alt + L

3. Select Font .... F

TIP

Instead of following steps 2 and 3, press **F9**.

4. Change Font Face .... Alt + F

5. **(Optional)** Change the point size of text .... Alt + S
   number or ↑ ↓

6. **(Optional)** Select from these options to change the appearance of text:

Bold .... Alt + B

Double Underline....................... Alt + D

Underline.................................... Alt + U

Italic .... Alt + I

Outline .... Alt + N

Shadow .... Alt + W

Small Cap .... Alt + C

Redline .... Alt + R

Strikeout.................................... Alt + K

7. Select **OK** .... ⏎

Fonts—Changing the Initial Font

Use this command to change the base (default) font for a document.

To change the base font for all new documents, open the File menu, choose Select Printer, and select Initial Font. Then start at step 4.

1. Open the Layout menu .... Alt + L

2. Choose **Font** .... F

Instead of steps 1 and 2, press **F9**.

3. Choose Initial Font .... `Alt` + `T`

4. Change Font Face .... `Alt` + `F`
   `↑` `↓`

5. **(Optional)** Change the Font
   Style .... `Alt` + `O`
   `↑` `↓`

6. **(Optional)** Change the Font Size
   of text .... `Alt` + `S`
   # or `↑` `↓`

7. Select **OK** .... `↵`

8. Select **OK** again .... `↵`

Footnotes and Endnotes— Creating

Use this command to create footnotes or endnotes in a document. Footnotes are references that appear at the bottom of the page on which they are referenced. Endnotes are like footnotes, but endnotes are placed together in some other location (usually the end of a section or chapter). Both footnotes and endnotes are marked in text with a number or some special character (such as *).

TIP

To see your footnotes or endnotes, use Page view. Select the **Page** command from the View menu, or press **Alt+F5**.

1. Place the cursor where you want to insert a footnote or endnote reference.

2. Open the Insert menu.

3. Click on either Footnote or Endnote.

4. Click on Create.

5. Enter the footnote or endnote.

6. Click on the Close button on the Footnote/ Endnote Feature Bar.

Footnotes and Endnotes—Editing

Use this command to edit a footnote or endnote.

1. Click on the Insert menu.

2. Click on Footnote or Endnote.

3. Click on Edit.

4. Enter the number of the footnote or endnote to edit.

5. Click on OK.

6. Edit the footnote or endnote.

7. Click on the Close button on the Footnote/ Endnote Feature Bar.

Form File—Creating

A form file is used as part of a merge operation (see "Document—Merging Data and Form Files"). Use this command to create the form file into which the data is merged, one set (or record) of data for each copy of the form created.

1. Click on the **Merge** button on the Merge Feature Bar.

2. Click on **F**orm.

3. Click on **New** Document Window.

4. Click on **OK**.

5. Enter the name of the file containing the data to be inserted into your form document.

 Click on the file icon to locate a file.

6. Click on **OK**.

7. Type your form document using the buttons on the Merge Feature Bar to insert fields where you want them:
   Click on the point of insertion in the form document.
   Click on **I**nsert Field.
   Select the field name you want from the Field Names list.
   Click on **I**nsert.
   Select **C**lose.

8. Continue typing the document, entering the appropriate fields in the places required using the procedure in step 7 as often as necessary.

9. When your form is complete, save it by clicking the **Save** button located on the Power Bar.

Grammar—Checking

Use this command to check and correct the grammar in your document.

TIP

WordPerfect checks your spelling, too, while it's checking your grammar.

1. **(Optional)** To check the grammar of a sentence or paragraph, select it first .... F8 , ↑ ↓ ← →
2. Open the **T**ools menu .... Alt + T
3. Select **G**rammatik .... G

MOUSE

Instead of steps 2 and 3, click the **Grammatik** button on the Power Bar.

4. Select **S**tart .... ⏎
5. When Grammatik finds an error, replace it:
   Select a suggestion .... ↑ ↓
   Choose **R**eplace .... Alt + R

MOUSE

You can also correct the entry manually by clicking inside the document, making your change, and then clicking Resume.

6. **(Optional)** Instead of following step 5, choose from other Grammatik options:

Ignore **P**hrase—Ignores this problem .... `Alt` + `P`

Next **S**entence—Continues the grammar check .... `Alt` + `E`

Skip—Ignores the spelling error and continues .... `Alt` + `S`

Add—Adds this spelling to the dictionary .... `Alt` + `A`

Close—Quits Grammatik .... `Alt` + `C`

7. When Grammatik is finished, return to your document .... `↵`

Graphics—Retrieving

Use this command to import a graphic object from another file into your WordPerfect document. When you retrieve a graphic, it is automatically placed inside a graphics box. To change the style of the box, see "Graphics Boxes—Borders and Shading."

1. Open the **G**raphics menu .... `Alt` + `G`

2. Choose **F**igure .... `F`

MOUSE

Instead of steps 1 and 2, simply click the **Figure** button on the Graphics Button Bar.

3. **(Optional)** Select the graphics type
   from the List Files of **T**ype list box .... ⬆ ⬇

4. Type the file name .... *filename*

   ⏎

   Or

   Select a file name from the list .... Tab

   ⬆ ⬇

   ⏎

5. Select **OK** .... ⏎

Graphics Boxes—Borders and Shading

Use this command to select the border style of your box and add shading to its interior.

1. Click on **B**order/Fill on the Graphics Box
   Feature Bar.

2. Choose the **B**order Style you want.

Click on **O**ff to remove the border
entirely.

3. Choose the **F**ill Style you want inside the box.

4. Click on **OK**.

Graphics Boxes—Inserting

Use this command to insert a graphics box into your document. Graphics boxes can be used for images, charts, text, and math equations. They make it possible for you to change the size and shape of graphics images easily, or they can act as "placeholders" to indicate where a graphic belongs.

TIP

To insert a graphic file (a picture) into your document, see "Graphics—Retrieving."

1. Move the cursor to the desired location for the box .... ⬆ ⬇ ⬅ ➡

2. Open the Graphics menu .... Alt + G

MOUSE

Instead of steps 1 and 2, click the **Custom Box** button on the Graphics Button Bar.

3. Select Custom Box C

4. Select a style from the Style Name list .... ⬆ ⬇

5. Select OK .... ⏎

Graphics Boxes—Text Editing

Use this command to edit text in a graphics text box. To create a text box, see "Graphics Boxes— Inserting."

1. Click on the box to select it.

2. Click the Edit Box button on the Graphics Button Bar.

3. Select Content from the Graphics Box Feature Bar.

4. Select Edit.

5. Type or edit the text.

6. Click on Close.

Headers and Footers—Creating

Use this command to create a header (text that appears across the top of every page) or a footer (text that appears across the bottom of every page).

TIP To see headers or footers you must be in Page or Two Page View. (Headers and footers are not displayed in Draft View.) See "View—Changing Your View of a Document."

1. Open the Layout menu.

2. Choose Header/Footer.

3. Click on first or second header or footer.

4. Click on Create.

5. Type the text to go in the header or footer. ....*text*

6. **(Optional)** To include page numbering or other numerical designation, select Number and choose from among:

Page Number

Secondary Number

Chapter Number

Volume Number

7. Click on **Close**.

TIP

To discontinue headers and footers at some later point in your document, open the Layout menu, select **Header/Footer**, select a specific header or footer to discontinue, and then select the **Discontinue** button.

Headers and Footers—Editing

Use this command to edit a header or a footer.

1. Open the **Layout** menu.

2. Choose **Header/Footer**.

3. Select the header or footer you want to edit.

4. Select **Edit**.

5. Edit the text.

6. Click on **Close**.

Help—Accessing

Use this command to access WordPerfect's Help system.

To use a WordPerfect tutorial, select Tutorial from the Help menu. Then click on the arrow buttons to go from screen to screen. To select a different tutorial, click on Menu. To quit in the middle of a tutorial, go to the main menu and select Quit.

To use a WordPerfect Coach, select Coach from the Help menu. Select a task you need help on, and let the Coach show you exactly how to perform that task.

Get help about the WordPerfect feature you are using by clicking the question mark button on a Feature Bar.

1. Select Help ....`Alt` + `H`

2. Choose the type of help you want ....`↑` `↓`
   `↵`

3. To return to your document, click on Close or press ....`Esc`

Help—Locating a Specific Topic

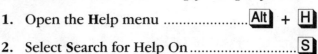

Use this command to access help for a specific task.

1. Open the Help menu ....`Alt` + `H`

2. Select Search for Help On ....`S`

TIP

You can also access Search from anywhere inside one of the Help screens.

3. Type in the word you want help on .... *text*

4. Click Show Topics or press .... ⏎

5. Select the topic you want to view .... ↑ ↓

6. Choose Go To .... ⏎

MOUSE

Instead of steps 5 and 6, simply double-click on the topic you wish to view.

Index—Creating

Use this command to create an index—a list of the topics covered and the page number(s) on which each topic can be found. First you'll mark the words or phrases you want listed in the index. Then you'll define the index style and generate the index itself.

Marking Text for the Index

1. Select the word or phrase you want to mark.

2. Click the **Index** button on the Generate Button Bar.

3. Click in the **H**eading text box to create a top-level heading in the index.

OR

Click in the Subheading text box to
create a second-level heading.

4. Click on **Mark**.

Defining the Index Style

1. Move to the end of the
   document .... `Ctrl` + `End`

2. **(Optional)** If you want the index
   to start at the top of a page, enter
   a hard return .... `Ctrl` + `↵`

3. **(Optional)** Type a title for the index ....*title*

4. Click on the **Define** button on the Index
   Feature Bar.

5. **(Optional)** Click on the **P**osition list box
   and drag to:

No Numbering	No page numbering
Text **#**	For example, Button Bar 7
Text(**#**)	For example, Button Bar(7)
Text **#**	For example, Button Bar 7
Text....**#**	For example, Button Bar.....7

6. **(Optional)** Click Use Dash to Show Consecu-
   tive Pages.

7. **(Optional)** To add or change page numbering options, follow these steps:

   Select Page **N**umbering.
   Choose **U**ser-Defined Page Number Formats.
   (Optional) Enter page number text.
   (Optional) Click on Insert and select a page number field.
   Click **OK**.

8. Click on **OK**.

Generating the Index

Anytime you make additional changes to your document, you should regenerate the index by following these steps.

1. Click the **G**enerate button on the Index Feature Bar.

2. Click **OK**.

3. Click on the **C**lose button on the Index Feature Bar.

Keys—Repeating

Use this command to repeat keystrokes, macros, and WordPerfect commands a specified number of times.

1. Place the cursor where you want
   to start the repeated action .... ⬆ ⬇ ⬅ ➡

2. Open the **E**dit menu .... **Alt** + **E**

3. Choose Repeat ....

4. **(Optional)** Specify the number of times you want an action repeated in the **N**umber of Times to Repeat Next Action text box .... *number*

5. Select **OK**.. ⏎

6. Perform some action.

Lines—Creating

Use this command to have WordPerfect create horizontal or vertical lines in your documents.

> **TIP** To edit a line after you've created it, see "Lines—Editing."

Mouse Steps

1. Position the cursor where you want the line to appear.

2. Click the **H Line**, **V Line**, or **Line** button on the Graphics Button Bar.

3. **(Optional)** If you clicked on the **Line** button, make selections and entries in the Create Graphic Line dialog box. Then select **OK**.

Keyboard Steps

1. Position the cursor where
   you want the line to appear ....

2. Open the Graphics menu .... Alt + G

3. Select Horizontal Line or
   Vertical Line .... H or V

> **TIP** To create a custom line, select Custom
> Line in step 3 by pressing **L**. Then make
> selections and entries in the dialog box by
> pressing **Alt** plus the underlined letter for
> the desired selection.

> **TIP** Instead of following steps 2 and 3, press
> **Ctrl+F11** to create a horizontal line, or
> press **Ctrl+Shift+F11** to create a vertical
> line.

Lines—Editing

*Use this command to make changes to your
graphics lines.*

> **TIP** To create a graphics line, see "Lines—
> Creating."

1. Position the cursor in front of
   the line you want to change ....

MOUSE

Instead of step 1, just click on the line to select it.

2. Open the Graphics menu .... Alt + G

3. Choose Edit Line .... N

4. Select either the Horizontal or
   Vertical option button .... Alt + O or
   Alt + V

5. Select desired options ...... Alt + *underlined letter*

6. Select OK .... ↵

Lines—Numbering

Use this command to number each line in a document.

EXAMPLE

In many legal documents, each line must be numbered so it can be referred to easily in contracts and other official papers.

1. Place the cursor where you want
   line numbering to begin .... ↑ ↓ ← →

2. Open the Layout menu .... Alt + L

3. Select Line L

4. Choose Numbering .... N

5. Select Turn Line Numbering On ..... Alt + O

TIP

To turn line numbering off later in the document, repeat these steps and deselect Turn Line Numbering **On**.

6. Change options as necessary:

Option	Allows you to
Numbering **Method**	Select from letters, numbers, or Roman numerals.
**Starting Line Number	Change the number WordPerfect starts numbering with.
**First Printing Line Number	Specify the first line number to print.
**Numbering Interval	Change the interval between line numbers.
From Left Edge of Page	Specify the distance between the line number and the edge of the page or column.
Left of Margin	Specify the distance between the line number and the left margin.
Restart Numbering on Each Page	Specify whether line numbers will reset at the top of each page.

Count Blank Lines	Specify whether to number blank lines.
Number all News-paper Columns	Number lines in newspaper-style columns.

7. Select **OK** ....

Lists—Creating

Use this command to create listings for figures, tables, charts, and other objects in your document. First, mark the text that describes each object you want to list (for example, each figure). Then define the list format and generate the listing.

Marking Objects for the Listing

1. Click the **T**ools menu.

2. Click on **L**ist.

3. Type a name for the list in the text box on the List Feature Bar.

For example, type **Figures Listing**.

EXAMPLE

4. Select the word or phrase you want to include as an entry in the list.

5. Click on **M**ark.

6. Repeat steps 5 and 6 for each item you want to include in a list.

Defining the Listing Format

1. Move the cursor to the end of the document .... `Ctrl` + `End`

2. Enter a title for the listing ....*title*

3. **(Optional)** If you want the list to start at the top of a page, enter a hard return ....`Ctrl` + `⏎`

4. Click the **Define** button on the List Feature Bar.

5. Select a listing from those displayed.

6. Click **Insert**.

7. Click the **Generate** button on the List Feature Bar.

8. Click **OK**.

Generating the Listing

Anytime you make additional changes to your document, you should regenerate the list by following these steps.

1. Click on the **Generate** button on the List Feature Bar.

2. Click on **OK** ....`⏎`

Macros—Creating

See "Macros—Recording."

Macros—Editing

Use this command to edit an existing macro. For information on running macros, see "Macros—Running."

1. Click on the **Edit Macro** button on the Macros Button Bar.

2. Enter the macro's name in the **Name** box.

    OR

    Click on the file icon, select a macro from the list, and then click **OK**.

3. Click on **Edit**.

4. Make any changes.

MOUSE

To insert new commands, click on Command Inserter.

5. Click the **Save & Compile** or the **Save As** button on the Macro Feature Bar.

6. Click on **Close**.

Macros—Recording

Use this command to record a macro. A macro is a set of recorded keystrokes. You can save time by creating macros that perform tasks you do frequently. You can also create macros to perform long and complicated tasks: just turn the macro on and do other things while it runs, and you won't need to worry about interruptions or errors. To play a macro after recording it, see "Macros—Running." To change the macro later, see "Macros—Editing."

TIP Assign your favorite macros to appear at the bottom of the **Macro** menu. Open the Tools menu, select **Macro**, select **Play**, choose **Menu**, and then select **Insert**. Type the name of the macro you want to add to the macro list, and then choose Select. Choose **OK** or add some more macros to the list by choosing Insert.

1. Open the Tools menu .... **Alt** + **T**

2. Select **Macro** .... **M**

3. Select **Record** .... **R**

MOUSE Instead of following steps 1 through 3, click the **Record** button on the Macros Button Bar or press **Ctrl+F10**.

4. Type a **Name** for the macro .... **Alt** + **N**
   macro name

EXAMPLE

For example, type **Insert Address**.

5. Select **Record** again .... ⏎

6. Perform the steps to record.

7. Turn off the recorder by clicking on
   the **Record** button on the Macros
   Button Bar or by pressing .... **Ctrl** + **F10**

Macros—Running

Use the Macro Play command to run a previously recorded macro.

1. Select the Tools menu .... **Alt** + **T**

2. Select **Macro** .... **M**

3. Select **Play** .... **P**

MOUSE

Instead of following steps 1 through 3, click the **Play** button on the Macros Button Bar or press **Alt+F10**.

4. Type the name of the macro you want
   to run .... ***macro name***

   OR

   Click the file icon, select a macro, and click
   OK.

5. Select **Play** .... ⏎

Margins—Changing for the Current Document

Use the following command to set new margins for the current document only.

Mouse Steps

1. Click at the point in the document where you would like the new margins to take effect.

To change the margins throughout the document, move to the beginning of the document by pressing **Ctrl+Home**.

You can also click the right mouse button in the margin to access a special QuickMenu from which you can select Margins.

2. Click the **Pg Margins** button on the Layout Button Bar.

3. Enter the measurements you wish to change.

4. Click **OK**.

Keyboard Steps

1. Move to the point in the document where you would like the new margins to take effect .... ↑ ↓ ← →

2. Open the Layout menu .... Alt + L

3. Select **Margins** .... M

TIP

Instead of steps 1 and 2, press **Ctrl+F8**.

4. Select the measurement you want
   to change .... Alt + L or R or T or B

5. Enter the new measurement .... *measurement*

6. Repeat steps 3 and 4 for other
   measurements.

7. Select OK .... ⏎

Margins—Changing the Default

*Use this command to change the margin settings
(default margins) for all new documents you
create.*

1. Select **Layout** .... Alt + L

2. Choose **Document** .... D

3. Choose **Initial Codes Style** .... S

4. Open the Layout menu .... Alt + L

5. Choose **Margins** .... M

6. Select a setting to
   change .... L or R or T or B

7. Enter the new measurement ....*measurement*

8. Choose **OK** ....

9. Choose **OK** again ....

Margins—Releasing Temporarily

*Use this command to release the margin tempo-
rarily to enter text into the left margin.*

1. Place the cursor at the beginning of a line or
    paragraph.

2. Choose the **L**ayout menu.

3. Select **P**aragraph.

4. Select Back **T**ab.

Instead of following steps 2 through 4,
press **Shift+Tab**.

These steps move the cursor one tab
setting to the left. Repeat these steps to
move further to the left or change the tab
settings with the Ruler Bar. See "Ruler
Bar—Using."

Menus—Customizing

Use this command to create a customized menu bar, or to edit an existing one. You can add or delete WordPerfect commands from menus, add a new menu, or add commands that activate macros or programs.

1. Open the File menu.

2. Select Preferences.

3. Select Menu Bar.

4. Click on Create, or select an existing menu bar and click on Edit.

5. **(Optional)** If you choose Create, enter a New Menu Bar Name and click OK.

6. Select an option:

   Activate a Feature
   > Select a Feature Category.
   > Select a Feature from the list.
   > Drag that feature to an existing menu.
   > Release the mouse button.

   Play a Keyboard Script
   > Enter script text.
   > Click Add Script. (Script is added as a new menu.)
   > **(Optional)** Drag the script name off the menu bar and onto an existing menu.

Launch a Program

>Click **S**elect File.
>Select a program to launch as a command.
>Click **OK**. (Program is added as a new
>menu.)**(Optional)** Drag the program name
>off the menu bar and onto an existing
>menu.

Play a **M**acro

>Click **A**dd Macro.
>Select a macro to launch as a command.
>Click **OK**. (Macro is added as a new
>menu.)**(Optional)** Drag macro name off
>the menu bar and onto an existing menu.

7. **(Optional)** Add new menus by dragging the
    menu icon onto the menu bar.

8. **(Optional)** Add a line to separate commands
    by dragging the separator icon onto a menu.

MOUSE

You can move existing commands by
dragging them. To delete an unwanted
command, drag it off the menu.

9. When you're finished, click **OK**.

10. Select the menu you want to use and click
    Select.

MOUSE

You can switch between menu bars by clicking with the right mouse button on the menu bar, and then selecting the menu bar to use from the QuickMenu.

11. Click **Close**.

Menus—Using

Use this command to open a WordPerfect menu and select a command. See also "QuickMenus—Using."

TIP

You can remove the menu bar, button bars, feature bars, etc., from the screen by pressing **Alt+Shift+F5**. (If a dialog box is diplayed, press **Enter** to continue.) To redisplay the menu bar, etc., press **Escape**.

Mouse Keys

1. Open a menu by clicking on it.

2. With the menu open, choose a command from the menu by clicking on it.

MOUSE

You can select a command in one movement by clicking to open a menu, dragging the mouse pointer down the list to a command, and releasing the mouse button.

Keyboard Steps

1. Open a menu .... Alt + *underlined letter*

2. Choose a command from
   the menu ....*underlined letter*

TIP

You can also select commands by high-
lighting the desired command name using
the arrow keys and then pressing **Enter**.

Outlines—Creating

*Use this command to create an outline, or to
change existing headings into an outline so you can
easily restructure your document.*

1. Click on the **T**ools menu.

2. Click on **O**utline.

3. Select an outline style from the Outline
   Definitions list box on the right-hand
   side of the Outline Feature Bar.

EXAMPLE

For example, Paragraph style results in an
outline that uses numbers (1, 2, 3) for its
first-level headings, and lowercase letters
(a, b, c) for its second-level headings.

4. Enter text for the first level ....*text*

5. **(Optional)** To change outline levels:

   To next level .... Tab

   To previous level .... Shift + Tab

6. Repeat steps 6 and 7 for each item
in outline.

TIP

You can also use the Outline Feature Bar
to make changes to your outline. Use the
left and right arrows to promote/demote a
heading to a different outline level. Use
the up and down arrows to move a
heading to a different location within the
outline. To display only certain levels, click
on the appropriate number (for example,
click on **2** to show only the first and
second levels of your outline). Use the plus
and the minus buttons to hide/display
selected levels within your outline. Click
on **T** to change a text paragraph into an
outline heading, or vice-versa.

7. When you're finished, open the
Options menu and select **End Outline**.

8. Click on **Close**.

Page—Centering

*Use this command to center all the text on a page,
between both the left and right margins and the top
and bottom margins. To center a heading or a
paragraph between the left and right margins of a
page, see "Blocks—Centering."*

1. Move to the page you want
to center .... `Page Up` `Page Down`

2. Open the Layout menu .... `Alt` + `L`

3. Select **Page** .... `P`

4. Select **Center** .... `C`

MOUSE

Instead of steps 2 through 4, simply click the **Center Pg** button on the Page Button Bar.

5. Select an option:

Current **Page** .... **Alt** + **P**

Current and **S**ubsequent Pages .... **Alt** + **S**

TIP

To turn off centering later in the document, select **T**urn off centering at step 3.

6. Select **OK** .... ⏎

Page—Copying

See "Blocks—Copying."

Page—Deleting

See "Blocks—Deleting."

Page—Moving

See "Blocks—Moving."

Page—Printing

See "Document—Printing."

Page—Setting Size and Orientation

Documents may be printed on the paper with the long side vertical (like most portraits, letters, and books) or with the long side horizontal (like most landscape paintings, spreadsheets, and charts with several columns running from left to right). You can choose either orientation (and/or change the size of the paper you'll be printing on) using the following steps.

1. Open the Layout menu .... **Alt** + **L**
2. Select **P**age .... **P**
3. Select Paper **S**ize .... **S**

MOUSE

Instead of steps 1 to 3, simply click the **Paper Size** button on the Page Button Bar.

4. Select **P**aper Definitions .... **Alt** + **P**
5. Select the desired paper size and orientation from the list .... **↑** **↓**

TIP

If you don't find exactly what you need, create a new page size definition by clicking on C**r**eate, completing the required information, and clicking **OK**.

6. Choose **S**elect .... **⏎**

Page Breaks—Inserting

Use this command to force WordPerfect to begin a new page exactly where you want it.

EXAMPLE If you are assembling a cook book, you may want each recipe on its own page, even though some pages will be short. To accomplish this, insert a forced page break.

Mouse Steps

1. Place the cursor just in front of the text with which you want to begin the new page.

2. Click the **Force Pg** button on the Page Button Bar.

3. Select New **Page**.

4. Click **OK**.

Keyboard Steps

1. Place the cursor just in front of the text with which you want to begin the new page .... ↑ ↓ ← →

2. Create a forced (hard) page break .... Ctrl + ↵

TIP To delete a hard page break, turn on Reveal Codes (press **Alt+F3**). Then place the cursor just left of the code and press **Delete**.

Page Breaks—Keeping Text Together on the Same Page

Use this command to keep a specific block of text together and prevent it from being printed on separate pages.

1. Select the block of text you want to protect .... `F8`

   `↑` `↓` `→` `←`

2. Select the **L**ayout menu .... `Alt` + `L`

3. Choose **P**age .... `P`

4. Choose **K**eep Text Together .... `K`

Instead of steps 2 and 3, simply click the **Keep Tog** button on the Page Button Bar.

MOUSE

5. Select an option:

   Prevent first and last lines of paragraphs from being separated across pages .... `Alt` + `P`

   Keep selected text together on the same page .... `Alt` + `K`

   Number of lines to keep together ... `Alt` + `N`
   #

6. Choose **O**K .... `↵`

Page Numbers—Adding

*Use this command to add page numbering through-
out your document or on selected pages.*

TIP

If you want better control over where the
page numbers print on the page, or you
need to vary the text and page numbers
throughout the document, see "Headers
and Footers—Creating."

Mouse Steps

1. Place the cursor at the top of the
    page where you want page
    numbering to begin.

    OR

    To add page numbering throughout,
    move to the beginning of the
    document .... Ctrl + Home

2. Click the **Pg #** button on the Page
    Button Bar.

3. Select a **Position**.

TIP

To suppress page numbering later in the
document, repeat these steps and choose
No Page Numbering at step 3.

4. **(Optional)** Change the Font.

5. **(Optional)** To add a chapter or
    section number, click **Options**,
    select an option, and then click **OK**.

6. **(Optional)** Change the starting
   page number by clicking **Value**.

7. Click **OK**.

Keyboard Steps

1. Place the cursor at the top of the
   page where you want page
   numbering to begin .... ↑ ↓ ← →

   OR

   To add page numbering throughout,
   move to the beginning of the
   document .... Ctrl + Home

2. Select **Layout** .... Alt + L

3. Choose **Page** .... P

4. Choose **Numbering** .... N

5. Select a **Position** .... Alt + P

   ↑ ↓

6. **(Optional)** Change the **Font** .... Alt + F

   ↑ ↓

   ↵

7. **(Optional)** Add a chapter or
   section number .... Alt + O
   Select an option ..... Alt + *underlined letter*
   Select **OK** .... ↵

8. **(Optional)** Change the starting
   page number .... Alt + V
   number
   ⏎

9. Choose **OK** .... ⏎

Paper Size and Paper Type—Selecting

*Use this command to select the correct paper size
and orientation (landscape or portrait) for your
document.*

MOUSE

To create or print an envelope, click the
Envelope button on the WordPerfect
Button Bar.

1. Select the Layout menu .... Alt + L
2. Choose **Page** .... P
3. Choose **Paper Size** .... S

MOUSE

Instead of steps 1 and 2, simply click the
Paper Size button on the Page Button
Bar.

4. Highlight a paper size from those
   listed under **P**aper Definitions .... Alt + P
   ↑ **or** ↓

5. Choose Select .... Alt + S

Paragraphs—Copying

See "Blocks—Copying."

Paragraphs—Deleting

See "Blocks—Deleting."

Paragraphs—Indenting

Use this command to create an indent. An indent moves a paragraph an additional distance from the margins (either just the first line of a paragraph or all the lines). A special kind of indent is the hanging *indent, which is created when the first line of a paragraph is kept flush with the left margin, and the rest of the lines of the paragraph are indented from the left one tab stop.*

TIP

You can easily indent just the first line of a paragraph by moving to the beginning of that paragraph and pressing **Tab**.

TIP

You can adjust the tab stops used to create indents with the Ruler Bar. See "Ruler Bar—Using."

Mouse Steps

1. Move to the beginning of the paragraph you want to indent.

2. Click on any of these buttons located on the Layout Button Bar:

Indent	Indents all lines one tab stop from the left margin.
LR Indent	Indents all lines one tab stop from the left and right margins.
Hanging Ind	Creates a hanging indent.

Keyboard Steps

1. Move to the beginning of the paragraph you want to indent .... `Ctrl` + `↑`

2. Select an indent option:

Indent—Indents all lines one tab stop from the left margin .... `F7`

LR Indent—Indents all lines one tab stop from the left and right margins .... `Ctrl` + `Shift` + `F7`

Hanging Ind—Creates a hanging indent .... `Ctrl` + `F7`

Paragraphs—Moving

See "Blocks—Moving."

Paragraphs—Sorting

See "Document—Sorting Text Within."

Power Bar—Using

Use this command to access and customize the Power Bar.

Displaying the Power Bar

1. Open the View menu.

2. Select Power Bar.

Selecting a Command Button

To select a command, click on its button on the Power Bar.

Customizing the Power Bar

1. Click the right mouse button on the Power Bar.

2. Select Preferences from the QuickMenu.

3. (Optional) To add new buttons to the Power Bar, click on an item in the Items list box.

4. (Optional) To delete a button from the Power Bar, drag the button off the bar.

5. (Optional) To move a button, drag it to its new location on the Power Bar.

6. (Optional) Separate buttons by dragging the Separator icon onto the Power Bar.

7. Click OK.

Printer—Installing

Use this command to install a new printer for WordPerfect. When you "install" a printer, you are really adding a printer file (called a printer driver) *to the WordPerfect directory. This file contains information about the printer so WordPerfect can communicate with it.*

TIP

You can also use Windows printer drivers with WordPerfect (and any other Windows program). To install a new Windows printer driver, consult your Windows documentation.

1. Open the File menu .... Alt + F

2. Choose Select Printer L

3. Select Add Printer .... Alt + A

4. Select WordPerfect .... P

5. Select a printer from the Printers list ..... ↑ ↓

6. (Optional) If your printer is not listed, select Additional Printers ...... Alt + D

   Then select a printer .... ↑ ↓

7. Select OK .... ↵

8. Confirm the printer driver file name .... *filename*

   Select OK .... ↵

9. (Optional) Begin using the new printer .... Alt + S

Printer—Selecting

If you have more than one printer installed, you can select a different one to use before you print. Use this command to select a printer.

TIP

You can also switch printers from within the Print dialog box by choosing **S**elect. See "Document—Printing."

1. Open the File menu ....`Alt` + `F`

2. Choose Select Printer ....`L`

3. Select a printer ....`↑` or `↓`

4. Choose Select ....`↵`

QuickFinder—Creating an Index

Use this command to create an index which speeds up searching through documents for specific text. See "QuickFinder—Using."

1. From within the QuickFinder dialog box, select Indexer ....`Alt` + `X`

2. Select Create ....`Alt` + `R`

3. Enter an index Name ....*name*

4. Enter a directory or file to add to the index under Add Directory or File ....*drive:\directory\filename*

5. **(Optional)**To include subdirectories
   in your search, select Include
   Subtree .... Alt + N

6. Select Add .... Alt + A

7. Repeat steps 4 to 6 for additional
   directories and/or files.

8. Select Generate .... Alt + G

9. Select Close .... Alt + C

QuickFinder—Using

*Use this command to search for a document based
on its contents.*

TIP

You can also select QuickFinder from
within the Open File dialog box.

1. Select the File menu .... Alt + F

2. Choose QuickFinder .... Q

3. Type the name of the file to search,
   or enter a File Pattern .... Alt + P
   filepattern

EXAMPLE When specifying a group of files to search (a file pattern), use wild cards, such as ? (which represents a single character) and * (which represents multiple characters). For example, mar* would match Mark, marquee, and marketing. Mar? would match Mark only.

4. Enter text to search for in the Search For text box .... Alt + S
                                                                    text

5. Select a Search In option: .... Alt + I
                                                                    ↑ ↓

    Directory—Searches just the directory

    Disk—Searches the entire disk

    Subtree—Searches the directory and any subdirectories

    QuickFinder Index—Searches indexed files

TIP If you often search for text within documents, you'll want to create a QuickFinder Index, and then select it in step 6. See "QuickFinder—Creating an Index."

6. **(Optional)** Enter a date range to search for or click the calendar icon

    From .... Alt + R
                                                                    date

To .... Alt + T

date

7. **(Optional)** Choose to search
   WordPerfect Documents Only .... Alt + W

8. **(Optional**) Choose from these
   Options .... Alt + O

choose a letter

Summary Fields—Search on
document summary fields .... F

Last Search **R**esults—Review the
results from the most recent search .... R

Clear—Clear selections C

Load Search Query—Use previously
saved query L

Save Search Query—Save selections
for reuse .... S

Delete Search Query—Delete a previously
saved query .... D

9. Select Find .... Alt + F

QuickFormat—Using

*Use this command to copy paragraph styles, fonts,
and other text attributes from selected text to other
text.*

1. Move the insertion point to the text whose
   attributes you want to copy.

2. Click the **QuickFormat** button on the WordPerfect Button Bar.

3. Select an option:

   Fonts and Attributes

   Paragraph Styles

   Both

4. Click **OK**.

5. Drag the mouse pointer over the text to which you want to copy the formatting.

6. Repeat by dragging over other text.

7. When you're finished, click the **QuickFormat** button again.

QuickList—Using

Use QuickList to find those files you use the most. QuickList can be accessed from within any dialog box that lists files, such as the Open File and Save As dialog boxes.

TIP

To use the QuickList once you've added entries to it, first select either Show QuickList or Show **B**oth from the QuickList menu inside a directory dialog box. Then either double-click on an entry to select it or press **Alt+Q**, highlight a selection with the arrow keys, and press **Enter** to select the QuickList entry.

1. From within a file dialog box,
   select QuickList .... Alt + L

2. Select Show **B**oth .... B

3. Select QuickList .... Alt + L

4. Select **A**dd Item .... A

5. Enter a directory or file name to add
   to QuickList, or click the file icon
   and select one ..... ***drive:\directory\filename***

6. Enter a description .... ***description***

7. Select OK .... ⏎

QuickMenus—Using

QuickMenus provide a fast and handy way to access often used commands with the mouse. QuickMenus can be accessed from different parts of the screen, such as the Button Bars, the Menu Bar, the Power Bar, scroll bars, the status bar, text area, and Selection Bar. Use this command to open a QuickMenu.

EXAMPLE After you select a block of text, you can right-click to open a QuickMenu that provides a list of often used text commands, such as Cut, Copy, Paste, and Delete.

1. Move the mouse pointer to an area of the screen.

2. Click the right mouse button.

3. Click on a command from the QuickMenu to select it.

Ruler Bar—Using

Use this command to change margins and tabs with the Ruler.

MOUSE

To display the Ruler, click the **Ruler Bar** button on the Layout Button Bar.

Changing Margins with the Ruler

1. Move the insertion point to the location within the document where you would like to change margins.

TIP

To change margins for the entire document, move to the beginning of the document by pressing **Ctrl+Home**.

2. Press the left mouse button and hold.

3. Drag the left or right margin indicator (black rectangle) on the Ruler to its new location.

4. Release the mouse button.

Changing Paragraph Indents

1. Move the insertion point to the location within the document where you would like to change indents.

2. **(Optional)** To change indents for certain paragraphs only, select them.

3. Press the left mouse button and hold.

4. Drag an indent marker (black triangle) to its new location.

5. Release the mouse button.

Setting Tabs with the Ruler

1. Move the insertion point to the location within the document where you would like to set tabs.

2. **(Optional)** To set tabs for several paragraphs, select them.

3. Click on the Ruler to set left tabs.

MOUSE

To change the type of tab, click with the right mouse button on the bottom part of the Ruler and select a tab type from the QuickMenu. You can also add a dot leader or remove all existing tabs with commands on the QuickMenu.

MOUSE

To delete a tab, drag it off the Ruler.

Screen—Changing Display Modes

See "View—Changing Your View of a Document."

Screen—Zoom

See "Zoom—Zooming In on Text."

Sentences—Copying

See "Blocks—Copying."

Sentences—Deleting

See "Blocks—Deleting."

Sentences—Moving

See "Blocks—Moving."

Spelling—Checking

Use this command to check your spelling in a document.

1. **(Optional)** Select the text you want to spell check.

2. Select the Tools menu .... [Alt] + [T]

3. Choose Speller .... [S]

(B) Instead of steps 2 and 3, click the **Speller** button on the Power Bar.

MOUSE

4. Choose Start .... [↵]

5. To replace a misspelled word with a suggested correction, select a suggestion or enter a suggestion in the Replace With box .... [↑] [↓] **or**

   [W] + *suggested text*

   Then select Replace .... [R]

6. **(Optional)** Select one of these other options:

Option	Result	Press
Skip Once	Ignores this occurrence of the word	[Alt] + [O]
Skip Always	Ignores all occurrences of the word	[Alt] + [A]
Add	Adds this spelling of the word to current dictionary	[Alt] + [D]
Suggest	Displays additional alternatives	[Alt] + [U]

7. Return to the document after spell check is done .... [Y]

Spreadsheet—Importing

Use this command to import data from a spreadsheet file, such as one from Lotus 1-2-3 for Windows or Excel. You can import part or all of a spreadsheet file.

TIP

Importing refers to reading the contents of a file from another program and placing a copy of the data in your document. Data imported from a spreadsheet file is not updated when the spreadsheet is changed. See "Spreadsheet—Linking" if you want the data to be updated automatically.

TIP

You can link only a specific part of a spreadsheet by indicating a range of cells in the **R**ange text box.

1. Move the insertion point to where you want the imported spreadsheet to appear.

2. Select the Insert menu ....`Alt` + `I`

3. Choose Sp**r**eadsheet/Database ....`R`

4. Choose Import ....`I`

5. Select **S**preadsheet from the Data Type pop-up list ....`Alt` + `T`

`↑` `↓`

6. Select **T**able, **T**ext, or **M**erge Data
   File from the **I**mport As pop-up
   list .... `Alt` + `I`

   `↑` `↓`

7. Type the drive, directory, and file
   name of the spreadsheet you want
   to import in the **F**ilename
   text box .... `Alt` + `F`

   drive:\directory\filename

8. Select **OK** .... `⏎`

Spreadsheet—Linking

*Use this command to link data from a spreadsheet
file. Data linked from a spreadsheet file is updated
automatically when the spreadsheet is changed.
You can link part or all of a spreadsheet file. For
information on importing spreadsheet information,
see "Spreadsheet—Importing."*

> **✓**
> **TIP**
> If you only want to link a specific part of a
> spreadsheet, indicate the range of cells in
> the **R**ange text box.

1. Move the insertion point to where
   you want to place the spreadsheet.

2. Open the **I**nsert menu .... `Alt` + `I`

3. Choose Sp**r**eadsheet/Database .... `R`

4. Choose Create Link .... $\boxed{C}$

5. Select Spreadsheet from the Data
   Type pop-up list .... $\boxed{Alt}$ + $\boxed{T}$
   $\boxed{↑}$ $\boxed{↓}$

6. Select Table, Text, or Merge Data
   File from the Import As pop-up
   list .... $\boxed{Alt}$ + $\boxed{I}$
   $\boxed{↑}$ $\boxed{↓}$

7. Type the file name of the
   spreadsheet you want to import in
   the Filename text box...................... $\boxed{Alt}$ + $\boxed{F}$
   filename

8. Select OK... $\boxed{←}$

Starting WordPerfect for Windows

Use this command to start WordPerfect.

1. Start the computer.

2. Start Windows by typing .... **WIN**

3. Double-click on the **WordPerfect for Windows 6.0** program group icon.

4. Double-click on the **WordPerfect for Windows 6.0** program icon.

Styles—Creating

*Use this command to create a reusable style. A style
is a collection of formatting codes that you can
quickly apply to text as a group. For example, you
could have a style called Title that makes text bold,
24-points high, and centered, in Courier font. To
learn how to apply your new style to text, see
"Styles—Using."*

TIP

If you have already formatted some text or
a paragraph in a style you want to save,
select it and choose **QuickCreate** from
the Styles List dialog box. QuickCreate
will note the formatting settings of the
selected text and save them as a style.

1. Open the Layout menu .... Alt + L

2. Select Styles .... S

MOUSE

Instead of steps 1 and 2, click the **Styles**
button on the WordPerfect Button Bar.

3. Choose Create .... Alt + R

4. Type a name for the new style in
   the Style Name text box .... Alt + S

   name

   ↵

5. **(Optional)** Enter a Description for the style.

6. Choose a style Type ....[Alt] + [Y]

[↑] [↓]

Option	Description
Character	Affects selected text or text you are about to type.
Paragraph	Affects the paragraph containing the insertion point or selected text.
Document	Affects all text from the insertion point to the end of the document.

7. **(Optional)** If you want to specify what happens when you press the Enter key, select one of these options:

Deselect the Enter Key Will Chain to command, and the Enter key will act as normal.

Select <Same Style> from the list to continue typing in the same style after you press Enter.

Select <None> from the list to discontinue the style when you press Enter.

Select a style name from the list if you want to switch to the selected style after you press Enter.

8. **(Optional)** Insert formatting codes
    and boilerplate text in the Contents
    box from the Styles Editor menus.

9. **(Optional)** If you are creating a
    paragraph or character style and
    you want certain codes to take
    effect when the style ends, select
    Show Off Codes .... 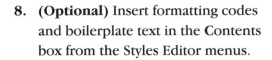Alt + O

    Then insert those codes in the
    Contents box .... *codes*

10. Select **OK**.. ⏎

11. Select **Close** .... ⏎

Styles—Deleting

Use this command to delete a style.

1. Open the Layout menu .... Alt + L

2. Select Style .... S

MOUSE

Instead of steps 1 and 2, just click on
the **Style** button on the WordPerfect
Button Bar.

3. Choose the style you want
    to delete .... ↑ **or** ↓

4. Select **Options** .... Alt + O

5. Choose **Delete** .... D

6. Select a delete option:

   Include Codes—Removes the style
   name and the style codes within
   the document .... [I]

   Leave Codes—Allows the codes to
   remain while removing the formal
   style name .... [L]

7. Select **OK** .... [↵]

8. Choose **Close** .... [↵]

Styles—Editing

Use this command to edit existing styles.

1. Open the Layout menu .... [Alt] + [L]

2. Select **Styles** .... [S]

MOUSE

Instead of steps 1 and 2, click on the
Styles button on the WordPerfect
Button Bar.

3. Select a style to change from
   the **Name** list.................................. [Alt] + [N]
   [↑] [↓]

4. Select **Edit** .... [Alt] + [E]

5. Use the Styles Editor menu to make changes
   to the style.

6. Select **OK**..⏎

7. Select Close ....[Alt] + [C]

Styles—Using

Use this command to invoke a style. You can turn on a style at a specific point so that it affects all text from that point on, or you can select a block of text first and apply the style to that block of text only.

Mouse Steps

1. **(Optional)** Select the text to which you want to apply the style.

2. Click the **Styles** button on the WordPerfect Button Bar.

3. Select the desired style.

4. Click on **Apply**.

Keyboard Steps

1. **(Optional)** Select the text to which you want to apply the style ....[F8]

   [↑] [↓] [←] [→]

2. Open the **Layout** menu ....[Alt] + [L]

3. Select Styles ....[S]

4. Highlight the desired style...............[↑] **or** [↓]

5. Choose **Apply** ....[Alt] + [A]

Styles List—Retrieving

*Use this command to retrieve a list of predefined
styles from an existing document so you don't have
to recreate them.*

1. Open the Layout menu .... `Alt` + `L`

2. Select Styles .... `S`

MOUSE
Instead of steps 1 and 2, click the **Styles**
button on the WordPerfect Button Bar.

3. Choose Options .... `Alt` + `O`

4. Select Retrieve .... `E`

5. Specify the document from which
   you want to copy the styles .... `↑` `↓`

6. Specify which styles you want to
   retrieve:

   Both .... `Alt` + `B`

   User Styles .... `Alt` + `U`

   System Styles .... `Alt` + `S`

7. Select **OK** .... `↵`

8. Decide whether to overwrite
   existing styles .... `Y` or `N`

9. Select Close .... `↵`

Table of Contents

A table of contents is used by readers to find topics in a book or other long document. Use this command to mark text for the table of contents, define the format, and finally, generate a table of contents in a document.

Marking Text for a Table of Contents

1. Select the heading you want to mark.

2. Click the **ToC** button on the Generate Button Bar.

3. Click on the **Mark** button containing this entry's level number.

4. Repeat steps 1 and 3 for each item.

Defining the Format of Your Table of Contents

1. Move to the place in your document where you want the table of contents.

2. Click the **Define** button on the Table of Contents Feature Bar.

3. Set the number of levels you want to include (1–5).

4. Select a Numbering Format for each level in the table of contents.

5. **(Optional)** Choose **P**age Numbering if you want to use volume numbers, chapter numbers, or page numbers.

6. **(Optional)** If you want the last level wrapped flush left, select **D**isplay Last Level in Wrapped Format.

7. **(Optional)** To change the style of the table of contents, click on **S**tyles.

8. Click on **OK**.

Generating Your Table of Contents

1. Click the **G**enerate button on the Table of Contents Feature Bar.

2. Click **OK** ....⟵

3. **(Optional)** If you want to separate the table of contents from the rest of the document, add a hard page break .... Ctrl + ↑

TIP

Anytime you make additional changes to your document, you should regenerate the table of contents.

Tables—Adding Rows or Columns

Use this command to add rows or columns to a table.

TIP

Columns and rows are added either before or after the current cursor position, and the new cells retain the formatting of the current cell.

1. Move to the cell next to which you want to add columns or rows .... `Tab` or `Shift` + `Tab`

2. Select the Table menu .... `Alt` + `A`

MOUSE

Instead of steps 1–3, click the right mouse button while pointing at the table, and select Insert from the QuickMenu.

3. Choose Insert .... `I`

4. Indicate whether to add Columns or Rows .... `Alt` + `C` or `Alt` + `R`

5. Select the number of columns or rows to add .... `↑` `↓`

6. Choose where to insert the columns or rows.

    Before Cursor Position .... `Alt` + `B`

After Cursor Position .... Alt + A

7. Choose **OK** .... ↵

Tables—Changing Column Width

Use this command to change a column's width.

Mouse Steps

1. Move the cursor to a border between columns.

2. Click and hold the left mouse button.

3. Drag the border to its new location.

4. Release the mouse button.

Keyboard Steps

1. Move to the column you want to change.

2. Open the Table menu .... Alt + A

3. Select Format .... O

4. Choose Column L

5. Increase or decrease width in
   the Width field .... Alt + T

   ↑ + ↓

6. Select **OK** .... ↵

Tables—Creating

Use this command to create a table. A table is a grid in which you can type data, much like a spreadsheet. For example, if you had many names and addresses to enter, you could separate the names from the addresses with tabs, but it would be easier to enter them into a table.

You can import spreadsheet data into a table, instead of creating one. See "Spreadsheet—Importing."

Mouse Steps

1. Place the cursor where you would like to insert a table.

To create a table from data that is already typed, select that data now.

2. Click and hold the **Table Quick Create** button on the Power Bar.

3. Press the left mouse button and drag to select the number of columns and rows desired.

4. Release the mouse button.

Keyboard Steps

1. Open the Table menu ....**Alt** + **A**

2. Choose **Create** C

> Instead of steps 1 and 2, press **F12**.
>
> **TIP**

3. Specify the number of columns and
   rows ....*columns*

   Tab

   rows

4. Choose **OK** .... ⏎

Tables—Deleting Rows and Columns

Use this command to delete rows and columns from a table.

1. Move to any cell in the table .... Tab or

   Shift + Tab

2. Open the Table menu .... Alt + A

3. Select **Delete** .... D

Instead of steps 1 and 2, click the right
mouse button while pointing to the table
and select **Delete** from the QuickMenu.

MOUSE

4. Choose **Rows** or **Columns** to delete
   entire cells .... Alt + R or
   .... Alt + C

Or

Choose C**e**ll Contents to erase just
the cells' contents ....`Alt` + `E`

5. **(Optional)** Select the number of
cells to delete ....`↑` `↓`

6. Select **OK**...`⏎`

Tables—Entering Data

Use this command to enter data into a table.

Mouse Steps

1. Click on a cell in the table.

2. Enter data.

3. Click on the next cell or on any previous cell.

Keyboard Steps

1. Move to a cell in the table ....`Tab`

2. Enter data ....***text* or *numbers***

3. Move to the next cell ....`Tab`

4. **(Optional)** Move to the
previous cell ....`Shift` + `Tab`

TIP

You can also press **Alt**+`↑` or **Alt**+`↓` to
move from row to row in a table.

Tables—Joining Cells

Use this command to remove the barriers between selected cells. This creates space for large data, such as a title that runs across the tops of all the columns in a table.

1. Select the cells to be joined .... **Shift** +
   ↑ ↓ ← →

2. Select the Table menu .... **Alt** + **A**

3. Choose **Join** .... **J**

4. Select **Cell** .... **C**

Tables—Lines Changing

By default, WordPerfect adds a thin line bordering all the cells in a table. To distinguish sections of a table or to add pizzazz, change the line style, color, or fill pattern of individual cells, or add a border around your table with this command.

1. Select the cells to be changed.

2. Click the **TblLineFill** button on the Tables Button Bar.

3. Select a Line Style.

TIP

To add a border around the entire table, click on Table and select a Border pattern.

4. **(Optional)** Change the line style Custom Color.

5. **(Optional)** Fill the cells with a grayed Fill Style.

6. **(Optional)** Change the color of the fill pattern by changing the Foreground and/or Background colors.

7. Click on **OK**.

Tables—Math Formulas

Use this command to enter formulas into cells.

Each cell has a name based on its location. Columns are numbered A, B, C, and so on, and rows are numbered 1, 2, 3, and so on. The cell in the third column, second row of a table is cell C2.

1. Move to the cell where you want to enter a formula.

2. Click the **TblCellForm** button on the Tables Button Bar.

3. Enter the cell formula and press ....

Use + – * / to add, subtract, multiply, and divide. For example, to add the upper left cell to the one below it, type **A1+A2**.

4. Select Formula Bar from the Table menu for Options.

5. **(Optional)** Click Sum to total all the cells above or to the left of the current cell.

6. **(Optional)** Click Functions and select a table function, such as AVE (average).

7. **(Optional)** Click Copy Formula to copy formulas from cell to cell.

8. Click Close.

MOUSE

To recalculate your results, click Calculate.

Tables—Number Format

Each cell is set to accept data formatted in a particular way. Use this command to change the way data is formatted in a cell.

1. Move to the cell whose type you want to change .... Tab **or**

Shift + Tab

2. Select Table .... A

3. Choose Number Type .... U

TIP

Instead of steps 2 and 3, press **Alt+F12**.

MOUSE

Instead of steps 2 and 3, click the **Tbl #
Type** button on the Tables Button Bar.

4. Choose whether to format the
current **Cell** or **Column** or the
entire **Table** .... C or O or T

5. Select an Available Type from
the list:

Accounting .... Alt + A

Commas .... Alt + M

Currency .... Alt + R

Date/Time .... Alt + D

Fixed .... Alt + F

General .... Alt + G

Integer .... Alt + I

Percent .... Alt + P

Scientific .... Alt + S

Text .... Alt + X

6. Select **OK** .... ⏎

Tables—Position

*Use this command to change the position of a table
on the page.*

1. Select the entire table.

2. Click on the table and hold down the left mouse button.

3. Drag the table to its new position within the document.

4. Release the mouse button.

Tables—Removing

Use this command to remove a table.

1. Select the entire table .... `Shift` + `F8`
   `Shift` + `↑` `↓` `←` `→`

2. Press .... `Delete`

3. Select Entire Table .... `Alt` + `E`

4. Choose **OK** .... `↵`

Tables—Row Height Changing

Use this command to change the height of a row.

TIP

WordPerfect automatically adjusts row height to accommodate the largest font size used in a row, so you don't have to adjust for that. However, you might want to increase the height of a row so extra blank space appears above the row.

1. Move to the row you want to change .... Alt + ↑ or
   Alt + ↓
2. Open the Table menu .... Alt + A
3. Choose Format .... O

TIP

Instead of steps 2 and 3, press **Ctrl+F12**.

MOUSE

Instead of steps 2 and 3, click the **Format Tbl** button on the Tables Button Bar.

4. Choose Row .... Alt + O
5. Choose Fixed .... Alt + X
6. Enter a height measurement .... *height*
7. Select **OK** .... ↵

Tables—Splitting Cells

Use this command to split a cell into multiple cells. To join multiple cells into a single cell, see "Tables—Joining Cells."

Mouse Steps

1. Move to the cell you want to split.

2. Click the right mouse button.

3. Select **Sp**lit Cell from the QuickMenu.

4. Click on **C**olumns or **R**ows.

5. Click on the number of columns or rows.

6. Click on OK.

Keyboard Steps

1. Move to the cell you want
   to split .... `Tab` or `Shift` + `Tab`

2. Open the **T**able menu .... `Alt` + `A`

3. Choose **S**plit .... `S`

4. Select **C**ell .... `C`

5. Indicate whether to split
   Columns or **R**ows .... `Alt` + `C` or
   `Alt` + `R`

6. Specify the number of columns
   or rows .... `↑` or `↓`

7. Choose **OK** .... `⏎`

Tables—Text Appearance

You can make the text in a table bold, italic under-lined, and so on—just like any other text. See "Fonts—Changing." To change the format of numbers within table cells, see "Tables—Number Format."

Tables—Text Justify

You can make the text in tables centered, right-justified, and so on—just like any other text. See "Text—Justifying."

Tables—Text Size

You can make the text in tables larger or smaller—just like any other text. See "Fonts—Changing."

Tables—Text Vertical Alignment

Use this command to change the vertical alignment of text in cells.

1. Select the cells you want
    to change .... `Shift` + `F8`
    `Shift` + `↑` `↓` `→` `←`

2. Open the Table menu .... `Alt` + `A`

3. Select Format .... `O`

4. Select a Vertical Alignment .... `Alt` + `V`
    `↑` `↓`

MOUSE

Instead of steps 2 and 3, click the **FormatTbl** button on the Tables Button Bar.

5. Select **OK** .... `⏎`

Text—Adding a Shadow

See "Fonts—Changing."

Text—Adding with Insert Mode

Use this command to add text by inserting it between existing text. As you enter new text, existing text moves to the right to make room for the new.

1. Move the cursor to where you want
   to insert text .... ↑ ↓ → ←

2. Enter the text .... ***text***

TIP

Insert mode is the default mode in WordPerfect for Windows 6.0. If you are in Overtype mode (see "Text—Adding with Overtype Mode"), press the **Insert** key to return to Insert mode.

Text—Adding with Overtype Mode

Use this command to add text by typing over existing text.

1. Move the cursor to where you want
   to add text .... ↑ ↓ → ←

2. Press the **Insert** key to change to
   Overtype mode .... Insert

3. Enter text .... ***text***

4. Change back to Insert (normal)
   mode of typing text ....Insert

Text—Bold

See "Fonts—Changing."

Text—Centering

See "Blocks—Centering."

Text—Centering Between Top and Bottom Margins

See "Page—Centering."

Text—Changing the Size Of

See "Fonts—Changing."

Text—Color, Applying

See "Fonts—Changing."

Text—Deleting

See "Blocks—Deleting."

Text—Double Underlining

See "Fonts—Changing."

Text—Flush with the Right Margin

Use this command to place text flush with the right margin. You can also center text between the margins, or justify it (force it to spread out evenly between the left and right margins). See "Blocks— Centering" or "Text—Justifying."

1. Select existing text to be realigned F8

2. Click the **Justify Rt** button on the Layout Button Bar, or press .... Ctrl + R

Instead of following step 2, you can also click and hold the **Justification** button on the Power Bar and select **Right**.

MOUSE

Text—Fonts Applying

See "Fonts—Changing."

Text—Hyphenation, Controlling

Use this command to turn hyphenation on or off within a document. When hyphenation is turned on, it takes effect when a word enters into the left or right hyphenation zone (an invisible "cutting off point" along the left and right margins). You can change the size of this zone to increase or decrease the amount of hyphenation within a document.

1. Open the Layout menu ....`Alt` + `L`
2. Choose Line ....`L`
3. Select Hyphenation ....`E`
4. Turn hyphenation on ....`Alt` + `O`

> **TIP** You can repeat these steps later to turn hyphenation off.

5. To alter the left or right hyphenation zones:

   Set the Percent **Left** field ....`Alt` + `L`
   number

   Set the Percent **Right** field ....`Alt` + `R`
   number

6. Choose **OK** ....`↵`

Text—Hyphenation Options, Selecting

Use this command to change the type of hyphen-ation for all documents.

1. Open the File menu ....`Alt` + `F`
2. Choose Preferences ....`E`
3. Choose Environment ....`Alt` + `E`
   `↵`

4. Choose **Never**, **When Required**,
   or **Always** ....`Alt` + `P`

   `↑` or `↓`

5. Choose **OK** .... `⏎`

6. Choose **Close** .... `⏎`

Text—Italics

See "Fonts—Changing."

Text—Justifying

Use this command to change the justification of text.

Mouse Steps

1. **(Optional)** Select the text whose justification (alignment) you wish to change.

2. Click on the appropriate justification button on the Layout Button Bar:

   Justify Left—Text is aligned with the left margin.

   Justify Rt—Text is aligned with the right margin.

   Justify Cntr—Text is centered between the margins.

   Justify Full—Text is spaced so it fits evenly between both margins.

Justify All—Similar to Full, but the last line of a paragraph is not spaced out to reach both margins.

MOUSE

Instead of following step 2, click the **Justification** button on the Power Bar and select the proper alignment from the displayed list.

Keyboard Steps

1. **(Optional)** Select the text with the justification (alignment) you want to change..........⌨F8⌨

    ⌨↑⌨ ⌨↓⌨ ⌨→⌨ ⌨←⌨

2. Open the Layout menu ....⌨Alt⌨ + ⌨L⌨

3. Select Justification ....⌨J⌨

4. Select the appropriate justification:

    Left—Text is aligned with the left margin ....⌨L⌨

    Right—Text is aligned with the right margin ....⌨R⌨

    Center—Text is centered between the margins...⌨E⌨

    Full—Text is spaced so it fits evenly between both margins.................................⌨F⌨

    All—Similar to Full, but the last line of a paragraph is not spaced out to reach both margins ....⌨A⌨

TIP

To justify all the lines in a paragraph quickly, press one of the following accelerator keys:

Left	**Ctrl+L**
Right	**Ctrl+R**
Center	**Ctrl+E**
Full	**Ctrl+J**

There is no shortcut for selecting All justification.

Text—Kerning

Kerning adjusts the spacing between letters to make lines appear neater and more professional. Use this command to turn word kerning on or off.

1. Move to where you want kerning to begin .... ↑ ↓ → ←

2. Open the Layout menu .... Alt + L

3. Choose Typesetting .... T

4. Choose Manual Kerning .... M

5. Set the maximum amount of kerning in the Amount field .... Alt + A
   number

6. Choose OK .... ↵

Text—Line Height

Use this command to change the amount of space, or leading, between lines of text. Leading is the spacing between baselines of text; using this command does not affect the size of text. To change the

height of text, see "Fonts—Changing." To double- or
triple-space text, see "Document—Line Spacing."

1. Move to where you want to
   change the line height .... ⬆ ⬇ ⬅ ➡

2. Open the Layout menu .... Alt + L

3. Choose Line L

4. Choose Height .... H

5. Choose Fixed and enter the height.............. F
   height

6. Choose OK .... ↵

Text—Redline

Use this command to redline existing text or text
you're typing. To compare two existing files and
mark additions or deletions, see "Document—
Comparing."

TIP

During the editing process, you can
manually add redlining to mark text you
want added to a file (strikeout text formatting is generally used to mark text for
deletion). After editing is complete, you
may want to update the file with the
indicated corrections. See "Document—
Comparing" for more information.

Mouse Steps

1. Move to where you want to begin redlining
   text.

2. **(Optional)** Select the text you want to redline.

3. Click the **Redline** button on the Font Button Bar.

Keyboard Steps

1. Move to where you want to begin redlining text .... ↑ ↓ → ←

2. **(Optional)**Select existing text to redline F8
   ↑ ↓ → ←

3. Open the Layout menu .... Alt + L

4. Choose Font .... F

TIP

Instead of following steps 3 and 4, simply press **F9**.

5. Choose **Redline** .... Alt + R

6. Choose **OK** .... ↵

Text—Removing

See "Blocks—Deleting."

Text—Replacing

Use this command to replace all instances of a word or a phrase within a document with other text.

1. Move to where you want to begin
   replacing text .... ⬆ ⬇ ➡ ⬅

2. **(Optional)** To search a smaller section
   of text, select it first F8
   ⬆ ⬇ ⬅ ➡

3. Open the Edit menu .... Alt + E

4. Select **R**eplace .... R

> Instead of following steps 3 and 4, simply
> press **Ctrl+F2**.
>
> **TIP**

5. Enter the text you want to find .... *text*
6. Type the replacement text .... Tab
   text
   ⬅

7. Select **R**eplace to replace this instance
   of the found text .... Alt + R
   OR
   Select Replace **All** to replace all
   instances .... Alt + A

8. Select **C**lose .... Alt + C

Text—Restoring Deleted Text

*Use this command to restore accidentally deleted
text.*

1. Move to the place where you want
   to restore the deleted text...........⬆ ⬇ ⬅ ➡

2. Open the Edit menu ....Alt + E

3. Select Undelete ....U

TIP Instead of following steps 2 and 3, simply
press **Ctrl+Shift+Z**.

TIP If your last action was accidentally deleting the text you want to restore, you can
use Undo to undo your last action. Click
the **Undo** button on the Power Bar or
press **Ctrl+Z**.

4. **(Optional)** To switch to another deleted
   item, select **Next** or **Previous**......Alt + N or
   Alt + P

5. Select **Restore** ....↵

Text—Searching

*Use this command to search for specific instances of
text.*

1. Move to where you want to begin searching
   for text.

2. **(Optional)** To search a smaller section of text,
   select it first.

3. Open the Edit menu .... Alt + E

4. Select Find .... F

TIP

Instead of following steps 3 and 4, simply press **F2**.

5. Enter the text you want to search for .... ***text***

6. To begin the search select Find Next or Find **Prev** .... Alt + F or

                                                            Alt + P

7. After the search, select Close .... Alt + C

Text—Small Caps

See "Fonts—Changing."

Text—Spacing

Use this command to change the normal amount of spacing between words and characters.

1. Move to where you want to change word spacing.

2. Open the **Layout** menu.

3. Click on **Typesetting**.

4. Click on **Word/Letterspacing**.

5. Select a word spacing option:

Normal—Let Windows set the spacing.

WordPerfect Optimal—Let WordPerfect set the spacing.

Percent of Optimal—Define your own word spacing.

To set manual word spacing, either enter the percentage of optimal spacing or designate the optimal numbers of characters per inch under Set Pitch.

6. Select a letter spacing option:

Normal—Let Windows set letter spacing.

WordPerfect Optimal—Let WordPerfect set letter spacing.

Percent of Optimal—Define your own letter spacing.

To set manual letter spacing, either enter the percentage of optimal spacing or designate the optimal number of characters per inch under Set Pitch.

7. **(Optional)** To adjust the spacing bounds for fully-justified text, enter the minimum percentage under Compressed To, and the maximum percentage under Expanded To.

8. **(Optional)** To manually set the leading (white space) between lines of text, click Adjust

Leading and enter a leading amount under Between Lines.

9. Click on **OK**.

Text—Strikeout

Use this command to strike out (place a line through the middle of) existing text or text you're typing.

TIP

During the editing process, you can use strikeout to mark text that you want deleted from a file (redline is usually used to mark text for addition). When editing is complete, you may want to update the file with the indicated corrections. See "Document—Comparing" for more information.

Mouse Steps

1. Move to where you want to change to strikeout.

2. **(Optional)** Select existing text to strikeout.

3. Click the **Strikeout** button on the Font Button Bar.

Keyboard Steps

1. Move to where you want to change to strikeout .... ↑ ↓ → ←

2. **(Optional)** Select existing text to
   strike out F8

   ⬆ ⬇ ➡ ⬅

3. Open the Layout menu .... Alt + L

4. Choose **F**ont .... F

Instead of following steps 3 and 4, simply press **F9**.

TIP

5. Choose **S**trikeout............................ Alt + K

6. Choose **OK** .... ⏎

Text—Underlining

See "Fonts—Changing."

Thesaurus—Looking Up a Word

Use this command to look up a synonym to replace a word or words in your document.

1. Select the word you want to look up F8

   ⬆ ⬇ ➡ ⬅

2. Open the **T**ools menu .... Alt + T

3. Select **T**hesaurus .... T

Instead of steps 2 and 3, simply click the **Thesaurus** button on the Power Bar.

MOUSE

4. Select a word from the list .... `Tab`

`Tab`

`Tab`

`Tab`

`↑` `↓`

`Space`

5. **(Optional)** To look up a synonym for one of the words in the list, select it in step and click **L**ook Up or press .... `Alt` + `L`

6. When the word you want is highlighted, select **R**eplace .... `Alt` + `R`

Undelete—Undeleting Accidentally Deleted Text

See "Text—Restoring Deleted Text."

Undo—Undoing Your Last Command

Use this command to undo your last action or command. To undelete up to your last three text deletions, see "Text—Restoring Deleted Text."

Mouse Steps

*Click the **Undo** button on the Power Bar.*

Keyboard Steps

1. Open the **E**dit menu .... `Alt` + `E`

2. Select Undo ....

Instead of following steps 1 and 2, simply press **Ctrl+Z**.

TIP

Windows—Arranging

Use this command to arrange the document windows that are open on-screen in either a tiled or cascaded manner. To open another document, see "Document—Opening."

Tiled windows form blocks that fill the screen, with no overlap among windows. Cascading windows overlap one another, with the title bar of each window showing.

TIP

1. Open the Window menu .... **Alt** + **W**

2. Select either Cascade or Tile .... **C** or **T**

Windows—Switching Between

Use this command to switch between open document windows. To open another document, see "Document—Opening."

1. Open the Window menu .... **Alt** + **W**

2. Select a document from the list .... **1** – **9**

TIP

If the window you want to switch to is visible, click on any part of it to make it active.

Word—Kerning

See "Text—Kerning."

Word—Spacing

See "Text—Spacing."

Word—Spell Checking

See "Spelling—Checking."

View—Changing Your View of a Document

Use this command to change your view of a document. See also "Zoom—Zooming In on Text."

1. Open the View menu .... **Alt** + **V**

2. Select an option:

    Draft—Does not display the entire document as it will appear when printed, but provides a faster working environment .... **D**

Page—Displays a single page as it
will appear when printed .... P

Two Page—Displays two pages side by
side as they will appear when printed .... T

MOUSE

You can display an entire page in Page
view by clicking the **Page Zoom Full**
button on the Power Bar.

Zoom—Zooming In on Text

*Use this command to enlarge text so you can see it
better, or to reduce text so you can see more of the
page.*

Mouse Steps

1. Click the **Zoom** button on the Power Bar.

2. Select an option:

   50%, 75%, 100%, 150%, 200%

   Margin Width—Text fills the screen.

   Page Width—The edges of the paper are
   displayed.

   Full Page—Text is reduced so a whole page
   can be displayed.

   Other—Enter a custom percentage
   and click **OK**

Keyboard Steps

1. Open the View menu .... Alt + V

2. Select Zoom .... Z

3. Select an option:

   50%, 75%, 100%, 150%, 200% .... 5 or
   7 or 1 or 0 or 2

   Margin Width—Text fills the screen .... A

   Page Width—The edges of the paper
   are displayed .... W

   Full Page—Text is reduced so a whole
   page can be displayed .... F

   Other—Enter a custom percentage .... O
   percentage

4. Select OK................................. ⏎

Index

G

T